A SEASON ORDERED BY THE LORD

Psalm 37:23:
"The steps of a good man
are ordered by the LORD."

COACH DAVE DAUBENMIRE

CONTENTS

FOREWORD

Sixteen years ago Coach Dave Daubenmire and I were united as teachers and coaches at London high School in London, Ohio. The journey that we have shared since that time has been an incredible trip, which will live with me forever. The one constant in that journey has been a common love for Jesus Christ, family, and kids.

The real journey began for us in the fall of 1990 when Coach Daubenmire shared with our team the vision of Romans 12:1-2. His mini-sermon that morning was a call to renew our minds as he urged us to no longer conform to the influences of the world. Little did I know what a powerful influence that five minutes would have on my life, and the inspiration that it would provide to call me to a closer walk with Christ. Thanks to Coach Daub and the Holy Spirit touching my heart, the last decade has seen me move from the back pew in the church to a current six-year leadership stint on our Church Council. As I watched Dave's faith walk, I was impressed by how closely his walk matched his talk. He is what I would call a "true Christian". Because of his call to renew our minds, the London Red Raider football program underwent a transformation from mediocrity to excellence. During the decade of the 90s we won six league championships, advanced to the state playoffs for the 1st time in school history as well as four more times, made a trip to the final four, and had two undefeated football seasons. Dave's record proves that during the 90s he was one of the top high school coaches in the state of Ohio. I believe that he never received the recognition that he deserved for his accomplishments, because people took for granted his outstanding coaching and motivational abilities.

In 1993 Coach invited my oldest son Jacob and I to attend a Promise Keepers event in Detroit, Michigan. This was a defining moment in our lives as the Holy Spirit touched us in a powerful way. I needed every ounce of faith from 1997 to 1999 as we stood beside Coach Daubenmire and his family as they were persecuted by an envious group of people who were determined to destroy all that we had accomplished. The Lord had used our time together to prepare me to stand for righteousness. Because of my relationship with Coach Daub, I was included in the suit brought by the ACLU. It was an honor to take a stand with his family against the pettiness of the parent group and the attempt by the ACLU to destroy this Godly family. I was privileged to be part of the ACLU depositions in the Daubenmire case, and I can assure you that the Coach shut out another opponent!

In 1999, our last season together, the Red Raider football team posted a 10-0 regular season record, and another trip to the play-offs, as our sons Jake, the center, and Zack, the quarterback, led us through this improbable season. Coming off of a 1-9 season the year before, we proudly tell folks that we went from "worst to first". There is no doubt that the Lord was in our huddle that year and that he honored our stand for the cause of Christ. What a blessing!

I consider it an honor to write the forward to this book. Coach Daubenmire had an unbelievable impact on many families during his time in London, Ohio. It is funny how God works. In an ironic twist, those who desired to silence Coach and his faith, had no idea how the Lord would use the events to propel Coach Daub to a far greater work. Thousands of lives, both young and old, have been touched by God's ministry through Coach since he walked away from coaching football. He now uses his time to coach God's team, and I can't wait to see the impact that he will have on this nation. He is a man of integrity who lives Biblical principles, and his passion for Christ is relentless.

—Coach Norm Emmets 2006

PREFACE

This book was written shortly after the conclusion of the football season in 1990. Much has transpired in our lives since then. In 1998 I was sued by the American Civil Liberties Union for praying with our football team. They claimed that our coaches were violating the civil rights of our players. After a two-year battle with the ACLU, our last football team having an undefeated football record, our family decided to move full-time into the battle for the Christian-American culture. We founded Pass The Salt Ministries, www.ptsalt.com and have undertaken the job of "coaching the church".

A Season Ordered by the Lord is a true story. Out of respect to their privacy, I have taken the liberty of changing the name of the young men who lived out this great story. I have left the story in its original form, as it was written in 1990, without the advantage of looking back over the next nine years at London, as a testament to the hand of the Lord being upon us at this earlier stage in London. No one could have predicted what would happen to us over the next decade.

London High School has a storied football history, but we are proud to say that we had the most successful decade in the history of the school. From 1990-99 we won six league championships, made our Ohio State playoffs 5 times, including a final-four berth in 1994, and had 2 undefeated seasons. Our 71 wins in the 90's is the most in any decade in the history of London High School.

This book is a tribute to all of the many players and coaches who made our success possible. Woody Hayes coined a phrase "You win with people." I would like to thank the Lord for all of the fine people he has surrounded me with.

All Scripture references in this story are taken from The King James Version of the Holy Bible.

Finally, I would like to dedicate this book to Michele, Zack, Abby, Maggie, and our dog Raider. No one will ever know what my family went through, and the sacrifices they made, as they stood with me against the forces of darkness.

"Romans 8:28 And we know that all things work together for good to them that love God, to them who are the called according to his purpose."

FLASHBACK

"Get the outside-linebackers wider," Mark Collier screamed into my headset. "They are just going to throw it out in the flat to one of the backs and we don't have anyone out there."

The thoughts were bouncing around in my head and I was doing my best to gain control of the situation. Our football team had just driven eighty yards to take the lead in our Central Buckeye League (CBL) championship game against the Dublin Shamrocks, and now the 'Rocks were staging a last minute drive of their own to win the game. We were clinging precariously to a 26-22 lead after rallying from a 15-0 half-time deficit.

The fact that we were even in a championship game was a miracle, truly the work of God, as London High School had come out of nowhere to challenge for the championship for the first time in fifteen years. With 4:34 left in the game, we had scored to take the lead, and now we stood helplessly on the sidelines as we watched Dublin move steadily down the field. With thirty seconds left and Dublin on our eleven yard line, our first-ever CBL championship seemed to be in jeopardy.

Our sideline was frantic and Coach Collier was screaming in my ear as we tried to come up with a defensive scheme that would halt this last minute drive.

"Korns needs to be wider, and so does Curtis," Mark screamed over the phones.

I was praying, as I always did throughout a game, and the commotion only seemed to be breaking the flow of my spirit.

"Tighten Carl up. He's giving up too much ground," Mark yelled.

I knew that the play on the field was out of our hands. We had prepared the team and it was too late for adjustments to be made. Coach Collier's exhortations were distracting, and they were irritating my spirit.

"Mark, just shut up and pray," I blurted out to him over the hum of the crowd.

His reply still echoes in my head.

"I already am."

The Vision

Habakkuk 2:2-3 "And the Lord answered me, and said, Write the vision and make it plain upon the tables, that he may run who readeth it. For the vision is yet for an appointed time, but at the end it shall speak, and not lie: though it tarry, wait for it; because it will surely come, it will not tarry."

Had it been up to me, London High School was not the place I would have chosen to go. For the previous eight years I had labored as head football coach at Heath High School in Heath, Ohio. Heath was a pleasant community and a great place to work. I loved the kids that I worked with and had developed some great relationships. My Mom and Dad were only ten minutes away, and we have always been a close-knit family. I had struggled for eight years to build a football program that we could be proud of, and the group that I had spent years nurturing had finally arrived at the high school. From all outward appearances, my future at Heath was rosy.

It was not something that I could explain to anyone. There

was a feeling inside me that I could not shake. At the age of 36, I believed that God's work in my life at Heath High School was finished. Ever since my spiritual rebirth the year before, there had been a tugging on my life that I could not pull loose from. I had discussed it with my wife, Michele, and we were totally unified in our desire to serve the Lord. Proverbs 14:12 says, "There is a way which seems right to a man, but its end is the way of death." No one could read my heart. After wrestling with it for weeks, the fact that a door was opening was made abundantly clear as we sat in the pew of World Harvest Church one January evening. World Harvest Church is a relatively young church that is located in Columbus, Ohio. Since it was started by Rod Parsley eleven years ago, it has grown to a membership of over 3500 members. It is non-denominational and free from the doctrine that is found in so many main-stream churches. The huge, circular sanctuary is splendidly decked in maroon and silver. It is filled with over two miles of pews, enough to seat 5200 for a Sunday morning, evening, or Wednesday night service.

In addition to the three weekly services, World Harvest has a national Television audience. Pastor Parsley's nightly program, Breakthrough, is seen on over 200 television stations nationwide. His message is clear and penetrating.

Since the night I had given my life to Christ, Pastor Rod Parsley, the anointed young preacher at World Harvest Church, had demonstrated to us Biblically that God is a man of His Word. In spite of all of the years of religious training that I have received from the Catholic Church, I had never been introduced to the true nature of God. How is it possible to truly have faith in a God whom we really don't know? My conversion had ignited in me a desire to more intimately know the God I claimed to serve.

This February night, as I stood at my pew, Pastor Rod read from a chapter of Habakkuk. As he shared the Word with us, he explained that he knew that there were many of us who had been praying for specific direction and that at times it seemed as if God wasn't listening. He challenged us to obey the Scriptures and directed us to imitate Habakkuk and write our vision on paper. As we stood together we asked the Lord to speak to us regarding our vision.

I took out an offering card from the pew and scribbled my prayer on the back of it.

"A new coaching job in a town where I can have a new start. In this town I will have a positive and dramatic impact on the lives of others."

Pastor Rod instructed us to stand and lift our petitions to the Lord and allow God to speak to us regarding our prayer. As I stood with my card lifted to the Lord, my right hand was suddenly filled with a soothing heat, as if I had inserted my hand into a hot tub. The warmth gradually flooded down my body and I could not have released the card out of my fingers even if I had wanted to. It was a profound moment.

As I walked out of church that night I didn't know where I was headed, but I knew I was leaving Heath. For the first time I understood what others meant when they said God had spoken to them. It was an unbelievable experience, something my Catholic upbringing had not prepared me for.

Things seemed to move quickly from there. Within a week I became aware that the head football coaching position at London High School was open, and I applied for it. I really didn't know anything about London other than a couple of college friends had lived there. God is amazing and He can use many different ways to speak to us. I'll never forget the day I knew I was going to London.

One sunny day in March as I was driving down the road in my silver Honda wagon, God gave me a glimpse of the future. As I was driving to my high school alma mater for an alumni basketball game, I was praying. I have learned that prayer is nothing more than a conversation with God, and I was talking to God much as you would a friend. I was thanking Him for all that he had blessed me with and for answering my prayer. I just told Him that I was anxious to hear where He was sending me so that we could begin making plans. That was it. Not some big in-depth, gut-wrenching prayer, just a conversation with God. As I finished I reached down and turned on the radio. The station was set on am880 WRFD, a Columbus-based Christian radio station. The first words I heard as the radio came on were clear and prophetic. "The Columbus Accuweather forecast for London and all of central Ohio is..." I nearly wrecked my car as the magnitude of what I had just heard settled in. I couldn't control my emotions. Tears filled my eyes as I realized the Lord had just spoken to me.

Needless to say, once God makes up His mind, nothing will change it. As I later interviewed for the London job it was incredible the amount of confidence that I had. I knew that God was placing me in that position and that the decision was out of the hands of the selection committee. Energy just flowed through me as the Holy Spirit directed me in the series of interviews. I didn't know if I was the man that the committee wanted, but I knew I was first on God's list. I told my family and friends that we were going to London. A week later I got the call.

There could not be two towns more different than Heath and London. Heath is a small central Ohio town 30 miles east of Columbus. The town was birthed in the late 1950's as an off shoot of an oil refinery. As workers began to locate in Heath, the community began to grow. In 1963, as a result of the Cuban Missile Crisis, a U.S. Air Force base was established in Heath. Seemingly overnight, the community of Heath exploded into a City of 8000 as civilian workers moved into Licking County from all over the country. Even though the community had grown, it had spent years trying to develop an identity. Because so many of the residents had moved in from other areas, a great deal of the residents did not feel loyal to the community. This lack of tradition made it difficult to build successful athletic programs. After eight years as Heath's coach, I finally felt we were getting the program positioned for success.

Although the population had not increased a great deal, the economic and industrial base had continued to expand. One of the first strip-malls in Ohio was built in Heath in the early 1960s and the rest of the town took shape around it. In 1986 a huge, modern indoor mall was built and further gave credence to the idea that Heath was not a town, but rather a series of stores. There is no such thing as downtown Heath. Once you are within the corporation limits, you find yourself in the midst of the hub of Licking County's shopping district. Only recently has the city of Heath begun to develop its own identity as the first generation of Heath graduates are now seeing their own children attend Heath schools.

London, on the other hand, is about the same size as Heath. It is located 30 miles west of Columbus and is the county seat of Madison County. Whereas Heath is only about 30 years old, London was established in 1881, and the appearance of the community of London took shape as an agricultural base for the many farmers in Madison County. It is the type of small community that many people would picture when they think of small town Ohio, complete with its own town square and county courthouse. London is surrounded by miles and miles of flat farming fields that for years were the means of support for a majority of Madison County's residents. Recently, as more families are leaving farming, the town has undergone a slow, painful transition to a more industrially based economy. London is populated with older, established families who have lived in the town for generations.

The largest employer in Madison County is now the Ohio Department of Corrections. London is home to two prisons. One is London Correctional; an older facility that houses about 1900 of the state's hardened criminals. It is an old, solemn looking facility that is a flashback to times past. The other prison is Madison County Correctional Facility. It is a modern, state-of-the-art prison built in 1985. It is set up in a campus style atmosphere in which its 2700 prisoners live in a dormitory type of setting. Whereas the older prison has high walls, the new one is surrounded by miles and miles of fence. The fact that the land around the prisons is so flat makes it very difficult for an escapee to hide and it helps the community to feel more secure.

Although London is only twenty-five miles from downtown Columbus and only six miles from Interstate 70, it is still able to hang on to its small-town atmosphere. As in years past, the high school and its athletic teams are of major importance to the city.

My first year at London, 1989, was the worst year of my life. I had heard once that we have to be careful what we pray for because we just might get it. That is the way I was feeling. My wife and I did not realize just how deeply our roots had grown in Licking County. We were homesick and our football season was a mess. I had inherited the coaching staff from the coach before me. They were all fine men and excellent coaches, but we were never able to come together as a coaching staff. For the first time in my life, I felt I had no credibility and that I had to justify everything that I did. Instead of the staff pulling together to solve the problems, we pulled apart. I don't blame anyone; it was just a situation that I had to go through. Romans 5:3 states "And not only so, but we glory in tribulations also: knowing that tribulation worketh patience, and patience, experience; and experience, hope, and hope maketh not ashamed." It was a year of spiritual pruning.

We struggled through a 3-7 season with a group that should have performed much better. During the off-season I determined that changes needed to be made, and I committed to having an entirely new coaching staff for the 1990 season. I didn't know who they would be, and I didn't know where they would come from, but I trusted in the provision of the Lord. I did the only thing I knew how to do. I stood on God's word. Philippians 4:19 says "But my God will supply all your needs according to his riches in glory by Christ Jesus." And Ephesians 3:20 "Now unto Him that is able to do exceedingly, abundantly, above all we ask or think, according to the power that works within us." I could not even begin to imagine what His hand would provide.

HELPMATE

Proverbs 18:22 Whoso findeth a wife findeth a good thing, and obtaineth favor of the Lord.

There are few families in the world that are more neglected than the family of the football coach. The coach's family has to take second place to booster meetings, film studies, speaking engagements, practices, and scores of other things that pop up unexpectedly. The job of keeping the family together falls unfairly upon the wife. Although I have prided myself on giving to my family, it is my wife, Michele, who is the glue that holds us together.

It is hard for me to imagine a prettier woman than my wife. She is a petite 5'4", 115 pound bundle of energy. If you were to see Michele, you would be struck immediately by her beautiful brown eyes which are outlined by dark, thick eyebrows. They make her small pug nose appear even smaller. Her smile is infectious and her enthusiasm is apparent. From the top of her dark brunette head to the soles of her small feet she is filled with the desire to love and serve others. I don't know why she got stuck with me.

We met in 1978 at Mt. Vernon High School. It was her first day of teaching, fresh out of Ohio Wesleyan University, when I set my eyes on her at the beginning-of - the-year teachers' meeting. My eye was caught by her physical beauty, but I was more attracted by something that told me she needed to be protected. We dated for 14 months and were married November 24, 1979.

It is amazing how God was working in my life even back then. Marriage was the farthest thing from my mind when I bumped into this sweet, young woman. God grabbed my attention, and I knew that she was the woman for me. We were both Catholic and enjoyed the same things. In over eleven years of marriage we have not had one serious argument.

We both loved Mt. Vernon, but in 1981, I got the opportunity to go to Heath High School as football coach. It was hard for us because we had made so many great friendships, but profession-ally, it was exciting to get such a great break. After shedding a few tears, we headed to Licking County and our new life.

Our first child was born to us on May 11, 1982. I knew that there had never been a child born like Zachary Charles Daubenmire. That, more than anything that had ever happened before, caused me to grow up and take full responsibility for my actions. He gave me a whole different perspective on children. For the first time I began to view my students as somebody's child rather than just someone I taught. I began to realize how special all life is.

Seventeen months later, Zack was joined by Abigail Anne Daubenmire, and the world's greatest rivalry was born. Every day of their lives has been spent in competition to try and establish the proper pecking order in the family. They have grown to love each other dearly, but love sometimes manifests itself in strange ways.

Our third and final child, Mary Margaret (Maggie) followed on December 2, 1987. She seems relegated to the role of baby of the family, and it is difficult not to spoil her.

We love our children beyond measure. We know that they are

a gift from God and we have dedicated ourselves to raising them in a Christian home from which we know they will do great things for God.

Michele has somehow held this family together. Over the years, I have coached football, basketball, baseball, wrestling, and little league baseball. I have been a basketball referee for eleven years and have taken part in numerous camps and clinics. During this whole time, she has been the constant. She has given her life to the raising and nurturing of our family.

If ever she was going to leave me, it would have been when we moved to London. Although God had spoken to both of us that it was time to move on, I don't believe that we were prepared for what lay ahead of us. Even though we had moved before, it couldn't compare to the shock of pulling up our roots and moving to Madison County. It was a long, painful year. Without our faith and knowing that we were where God wanted us, we would never have been able to hold it together.

The most disturbing part of the move was finding a place to live. We had sold our large 4 bedroom home in Newark at the last minute and had to rather hurriedly find a place in London. We were able to secure a 3-bedroom duplex in a nice neighborhood in town. It was nice, but small. Overnight our family had moved from a huge older home to an apartment where we literally had one room in which to live. The downstairs was one living area about 25 feet long and 10 feet wide. It was attached to a combination kitchen-utility room. All three bedrooms were upstairs. Our family existed for a year in these cramped quarters, and we lay in bed many nights and talked about once again owning our dream home. God is faithful, and a year later He provided us with a marvelous home. That is a testimony within itself.

The year in that duplex was almost unbearable for Michele. London is not an easy town in which to make friends. Although we had many acquaintances, no one really reached out the hand of friendship toward us. I was busy with my job, so I was able to handle it, but my sweet little wife had no one but the kids and her undersized apartment. She was strengthened daily by her misery and came through the whole episode a much stronger person.

Michele is so sensitive and she wears her heart on her sleeve, but she is, above all things, fiercely loyal to her husband. It has not been easy for her to go to football games and listen to the fans yell slanderous things at the father of her children. It was made especially tough by the fact that she had no great friend upon whom she could lean. She weathered it alone.

Whatever becomes of me and of my children will be a direct reflection of the silent role Michele has played in this life of ours. Always supportive, always loving, always thinking of others first, that's my wife. God's hand-picked helpmate.

MERCY

Romans 5: "But God commendeth his love toward us, in that, while we were yet sinners, Christ died for us."

I cannot tell you the number of people who reacted negatively to my move. My family was very supportive, but other people told me horror stories about London. To the natural eye, it looked like a bad situation. I have always prided myself on my ability to work in tough situations. As a short, stocky man of 5'7", 180 pounds, I bear a striking physical resemblance to former baseball great Pete Rose. I am the epitome of the little guy who needed to be in charge. More than once I have butted my head against a brick wall trying to do more than one man can do. Only when I turned my life over to Jesus Christ did I begin to realize that there were some things that I couldn't do. I used to joke that there was only one thing that I couldn't do and that was sing. Years of coaching had given me a husky voice and ruined my ability to carry a tune. Christ had shown me many other weaknesses, and through admission of my own shortcomings, He had created strength. I was ready for the challenge.

If you are not a football coach, it is very difficult to understand the amount of time and energy required. It is a year-round job. The ending of the football season leads immediately into winter weight lifting sessions where next year's football team is developed. To be able to compete against the teams that we have to play requires dedication and commitment from a young man. This dedication is difficult to get even in a successful program, and London certainly was not that.

A quick check of the football history at London High School would show that there had been a great winning tradition. Unfortunately, the last successful football season at London had been in 1978 when the Red Raiders finished 7-3. As a result, our athletic teams consisted of a group of young men who had never in their lifetimes seen a successful London football team. It had gotten to the point where the football program was running from the past rather than building upon it. No matter how hard the kids tried, they seemed unable to live up to what their fathers, uncles and grandfathers had done. The easiest thing to do in a situation like that is to not commit. They wanted to do well, but the payoff did not seem to be worth the investment. As the old saying goes, winning is contagious. So is losing. Without a full coaching staff, the job appeared overwhelming.

One problem with the program that was obvious to me was the lack of trust. Athletically speaking, London had turned into a selfish place. This is not uncommon. Whenever a team is struggling for success, it is only natural for the athletes to begin to focus more on individual accomplishments. You can't always control the actions and efforts of your teammates, so it is easier to begin looking out for number one. In order for London football to become successful again the athletes needed to understand sacrifice and team play.

To further compound the problem, there had been no consistency in the coaching staff. In the 50 years from 1925 to 1975, London High School had had only 2 football coaches, Jacob von

Kanel and Jim Bowlus. Both had been very successful and were still legends in town. Things had changed, however, and I was to be the sixth football coach since them and the fourth in the decade of the 80's. As a result, the players had very little confidence in anything that any coach had to say to them. Although they never said it to me, I sensed a lack of trust, and a feeling that they had heard all of this commitment stuff before. Until I could convince them that I was going to stay in London and that I could be trusted, nothing would ever be accomplished. Trust takes time. It must be earned, and these kids weren't about to let their guard down.

The winter weight program was a bust. Although I ran the program all winter, our attendance was at an all-time low. Enthusiasm was tough to generate, and I knew the kids were afraid that I was a phony. I had not hid my Christianity from them, and they searched my every move for any sign of hypocrisy. With no staff and no one to reassure the kids that I could be trusted, it was a long, seemingly fruitless winter. I had tried different types of activities to get the team together so that we could begin to bond, but nothing seemed to be of any effect.

In June, as school was letting out, I invited the seniors-to-be to my apartment so that we could plan a senior camp-out. The goal was to get everyone together and discuss the upcoming summer conditioning program and plans for the season. Although the seniors were a great group of kids, they were not a close knit bunch. Many of them were close friends, a mixture of small cliques, and fine young men. One thing was certain. They were not sure about this new coach. I needed to somehow win them over. Hopefully, during the camp-out we would be able to begin building a solid relationship. Little did I know that Satan would rear his ugly head.

I had learned through the Bible that Satan is alive and well on planet earth. Even though I had spent the first 34 years of my life in church, I had never been told that Satan was out to destroy my life. I believed that whatever happened to me, good or bad, was God's plan for my life. I wonder now, how many people still hold the same view as I did.

How is it possible to love and serve a God who seems to sit on His throne and arbitrarily bless and curse people? To many, getting God's blessing seems to be like playing the lottery. If you are in the right place at the right time and are a real good person, maybe God will throw a blessing your way. That is, of course, if He feels like it.

If God is real, then so is Satan. James 1:17 says "Every good and every perfect gift is from above," It doesn't say anything about bad gifts. God doesn't give evil gifts to His kids. Many of the bad things that happen to us are a result of our own sinful actions, the co-lateral damage from the sins of others, or the natural consequences of life on earth. Many, however, are the supernatural interference of Satan in our life. John 10:10 says "The thief cometh not but for to kill and to steal and to destroy: but I am come that you might have life and that they might have it more abundantly." It is simple. God is good, Satan is bad. God loves you, the devil hates you. How have we gotten it so mixed up? Why do we blame God for the things that Satan does? When I finally realized that Satan was out to destroy me that he was daily trying to mess me up, I was able to formulate a battle plan to neutralize his attacks upon my life.

On one June night at a camp-out in Springfield, Ohio, he dealt me a blow that would take every bit of faith that I had to overcome.

Our camping trip started out harmlessly enough. Eleven members of the senior class and I headed to Buck Creek, a state park in Springfield, about 25 miles from London. It has a large lake that is great for any type of water activity. Like all Ohio State Parks, it has several different camping areas. We selected an area that was in a remote area, where we would be free to make a little bit of noise without disturbing neighbors. It was a warm June day, and nature was emerging from a long, cold winter. The camp area was surrounded by trees and underbrush and it really gave us the feeling that we were roughing it. We pitched four different tents in an area about 100 feet square. A mild breeze carried the aroma of hot dogs from the campfires down the road. We spent the afternoon swimming, fishing, and relaxing.

This was a great group of young men. Ben Stronger was a 5'10", 185 pound guard and defensive lineman. He would eventually be elected co-captain of our team. Ben was a great leader. He was class president, student council president, and had ambitions of going to one of the military academies. Ben's red, flat-top and lightly- freckled face made him a natural soldier. He was one of those rare people who can be friends with all groups of people.

Joe Branson, the quarterback, was 5'10", 170 pounds, blonde hair, blue eyes, and hard working. He had been our quarterback since mid-way through his sophomore year. He was an excellent student and one of the hardest working, most reliable young men I have ever coached. He would be voted the other captain. Although Joe was well liked by his teammates, he tended to be somewhat of a loner, appearing to not have any one great friend.

Aaron Clymer, our center, was 6', 180 pounds. He was cut in the same mold as Ben and Joe. He had a light complexion with curly blonde hair. "A", as his teammates called him, was in the National Honor Society and was destined to be one of the leaders in his community. Aaron tended to run in the same circles with Ben Stronger.

Bill Kellmer, 5'7", 145 pounds with black hair and brown eyes, was one of the fiercest football players I have ever coached. Because of his size, it was difficult to find a place for him to play, but he was a coach's player, the type of guy who would do anything to win.

Doug Browning, called "Fresh" by his buddies, was 5'10", 160 pound defensive back. Doug's coal black hair and deeply set brown eyes gave him a sensitive appearance that made him easy to like. Like Bill Kellmer, Doug said little, but delivered a lot.

Zach Korns was another one of those boys who didn't say much. At 6', 170 pounds, Zach had played several different positions for us. He was a deep thinker, but kept most of the thoughts to himself. His slight build belied his strength. Bill, Doug and Zach are good buddies and one of the cliques on the team.

Chad Teeler was thickly muscled, 6', 210 pounds. He did not play football as a junior, but had returned to the fold for his senior year. Called "Biff" by his classmates, he was easy going and well mannered. Chad had moved from one group of friends to another. Like so many other high school kids, his strongest relationship was with his girlfriend, and that tended to cut into hanging-out time with his buddies.

Mike Fishman was a 5'10", 195 pound fullback and linebacker. He had a bulldog attitude and a gruff manner, being careful not to let his guard down in front of his friends. Because of his strong will, "Fish" and I butted heads more than once, but I always respected his desire to win. His thick thighs and chest made him a natural fullback. Mike had short black hair and a square firm jaw. Like Chad, his best friend was his girlfriend.

Bryan Merker, 5'8", 180 pounds, formed the other half of our inside linebacking core. "Bubba" was strikingly handsome with his dark black hair and stocky build. He was one of the emotional leaders of the team, quick to anger and demonstrative in his actions. Bryan spent most of his summer playing baseball, so he had not spent a great deal of time with his teammates that summer.

Kenny Stamms and Aundrey Clapper were our twin offensive tackles. They had the classic love-hate relationship, and were fighting one minute and cruising around together the next. Kenny was 6', 225 pounds, blonde hair, blue eyes and light skinned. Aundrey was 6', 235 pounds brown hair, brown eyes and brown skinned. Later in the season "Drey" picked up the nickname "Ninja" because of his resemblance to the famous turtles. He was volatile and emotional, but a fine athlete for his size. Both were thickly built, powerful, and in need of self-discipline.

The task ahead was to mold this fine group of individuals into a team. The leadership core was there. We just needed someone to step forward.

After dinner we had made plans to sit around the fire and talk about what our plans were for the summer and just how we hoped to accomplish our goals. It is my belief that the first way to develop trust is through communication. I had hoped to build a rapport with these young men that would help give leadership to our team. Any high school team is only as good as the senior class. I knew it was important to gain their confidence.

After darkness had settled in, we gathered around the crackling fire and began to talk about the up-coming season. Things did not go well. Rather than discussing how we could get where we wanted to go, most of the meeting was spent in argument and finger pointing over the previous season. We discussed alcohol and tobacco use and the players' responsibility to their school and to each other. They were not interested in anything that I had to say and seemed to be humoring me. After about an hour and a half it became obvious that we were just spinning our wheels. I dismissed the meeting and most of them went off to a fishing hole that they had found earlier in the day. One of the guys asked if I would like to join them but I chose not to and went into my tent to pray. I realized that I had made an error by not praying before the meeting and asking the anointing of the Holy Spirit to come. As a result, a demonic influence had shown up and had sewn discord in our camp. I needed to pray and seek guidance.

After about 10 minutes in the solitude of my dark tent, lit only by the flicker of the flames from the campfire dancing on the walls, my spirit suddenly became alarmed. I couldn't quite discern the meaning, but I felt I needed to go join the boys as they fished. I hoped that perhaps we could pick up our discussion in a less formal setting. The fishing hole was about 100 yards from the camp and the path wound through some under-brush. As I made my way towards the boys, tree limbs swished across my face and roots jutting up in the path tripped me. I could hear the boys clearly, but could not see them as they were sitting in an area protected by thick area of 6 foot high reeds. After a few more steps, the thick brush parted, and I broke into a clearing. It was totally dark except for the light provided by a half-full moon. Silhouetted in the moonlight were the forms of 3 young men. I froze in my tracks. I saw a distinct glow of cigarettes sticking out of the mouths of the forms. As I stood there with a crisp cool breeze swirling around my suddenly slumped shoulders, I heard a voice from the water's edge.

"Hey. Anybody want a beer?"

My stomach dropped as the answer returned.

"Not now."

Gloom and disappointment swooped down upon me and dug its claws in. I stood frozen for a couple of more minutes and then returned to the camp to gather my thoughts. The darkness in the underbrush was matched only by the darkness in my soul. As the shadows of the flames danced against the tents I wanted so much to be able to discuss this over with someone, another adult, but there was no one but me. As I prayed for guidance, I could hear the group of fishermen begin to change locations. I got up from the fire and returned to the previous fishing hole, slid down the bank and retrieved an empty twelve-pack of beer. Anger swelled in my chest as I looked out across the deep dark lake, at a boat bobbing among the soft, rolling waves. One of the Fruits of the Spirit is self-control, and I stood on the freshly tramped weeds, opened up my heart, and called out for guidance. Christ poured out His Spirit upon me.

Down the roughly hewn path I marched, empty twelve-pack in hand, until I came to a clearing where the boys had stopped. I saw several cigarettes and perhaps a cigar flicker in the night. Who they belonged to, I really don't know as I believe the Lord did not want me to see. I spoke firmly and without emotion.

"Come on, guys. We're going home."

None of the boys spoke as they began to gather their poles and fishing gear. Ben Stronger passed by me, leaned over and breathed into my face.

"Coach, I didn't do anything."

"Maybe not," I replied, "but you let it happen. To permit is to participate. You're all guilty."

In silence we walked back single file and dismantled camp. I looked at my watch. It was 2:15. I called the boys together and said, "If one of your friends has been drinking, please do not let him drive."

We loaded up for the 30 minute drive home. The boys all tried to pile in other vehicles and leave me to drive home in solitude.

"I've got room for 3," I said.

With heads down and tails between their legs, they crammed themselves into my Honda.

As we drove back in silence, the only sound was the hum of the engine and soft, gentle breathing of the boys in the car. My mind raced with just how I should handle this situation. Should I take them all to the Police Station and have them undergo a breath test? Should I make them call their parents and have them come and pick them up? Should I just throw the whole bunch off of the team, make a point, and get on with building a program? The one thing I was sure of was that these were good kids, and somewhere we had failed them. I could not have imagined myself, as a high school student, smoking and drinking on a camping trip with my coach. I had too much respect for him. But that was the problem. They didn't respect me, the football program, themselves, or London High School. Could I just throw them out with the morning trash? As I pulled into the parking lot at London High School, I still did not know what I was going to do. I called upon the Holy Spirit to send me His wisdom.

I gathered this miss-guided group in the dimly-lit gym and watched them spread themselves out across the floor as if wanting to distance themselves from the situation. I began to give the tongue-lashing that they all knew they deserved. For the year that I had been at London I had prided myself on my ability to control my anger. I rarely raised my voice in anger and tried to discipline them through love and positive reinforcement. I believe that the football players viewed this as a weakness and did not realize the amount of strength it took to control my temper. To them, anger was power. I tried to live by another set of rules.

For the next 5 minutes they saw the old Dave Daubenmire. I screamed and hollered and ranted and raved about what they had done as they lay motionless upon the cold wax-covered gym floor. My voice reverberated around the red and white painted gym as I blasted them for their lack of respect for me and for each other as my frustration spilled out upon the gymnasium floor. When I completed my tirade, I went over and sat down on the front step of the bleachers. I looked up to see the boys staring at the floor in a mixture of shame and disgust. It was then that the peace of Jesus Christ which passes all understanding came upon me and I began to speak from my heart.

I slowly stood to my feet and shared with them the miracle of salvation and just what Jesus Christ had done in my own life. How He had taken me, a common sinner, and had granted to me the mercy that only He could give. I shared that I was not a perfect person, nor had I ever claimed to be, but Jesus Christ had extended His boundless love and forgiveness toward me. He washed me in His blood and made a new creature out of me. I shared with them 2 Corinthians 5:17 "Therefore if any man be in Christ, he is a new creature; old things are passed away; behold all things are become new." I explained to them that mercy is an undeserved pardon of sins. God had freely bestowed upon me a forgiveness of my sins that I did not deserve. Since I didn't deserve the Grace Christ had extended to me, I felt that I had no choice but to grant to them the same type of undeserved forgiveness that I had received. Christ forgave me, therefore I forgive them.

The room was still as I shared my testimony. Some of the boys stared at the darkened ceiling, while others buried their head in their arms as they lay face down on the cool hardwood floor.

I spoke to them of their need to become the leaders of our school and how Satan had subtly convinced them that they were somehow unworthy and of no special value. I challenged them to do as 2 Corinthians 6:17 teaches. "Come out from among them and be ye separate." That they were, in fact, special, and all that they needed to do was to commit to God, themselves, and each other. If they would dedicate themselves to being all that God wanted them to be, they would be amazed at what God would help them do. The choice was simple, but the price would be high.

Dan Younger finally broke the silence.

"Coach, some of us made an agreement on the way back that we were going to stop doing this stuff."

"Yeah," Bryan Merker chipped in. "I know some of these guys would be in serious trouble if their parents found out. For the first time I think I realize how my actions affect others. I'm committing to this team. I'm with you, Ben."

Before I left the room I asked them to take a few minutes and make that commitment to each other.

"All you have is your word. If you can't stand by your word to your teammates, then don't make that commitment. If you say you've changed your ways, and then you don't, you have only proven to your friends that you can't be trusted. I'll be back in a couple of minutes. Do what you think is right for you, not what is popular."

When I returned, we made camp in the balcony that overlooks the gym floor. We pulled down the big mats that serve as high-jump landing pads during track season and the boys sprawled out across the balcony two and three people per mat. In an attempt to darken the room, one of the boys covered the ever-lit exit sign with a cardboard box. I lay down on a wrestling mat, curled up in my sleeping bag, and stared at the dust hanging from the rafters above my head. Sleep did not come easy.

The next morning we were awakened by the sound of a basketball being dribbled. Our basketball coach, Dave Gustin, was conducting a summer basketball camp and was surprised to find us there. We packed up and prepared to go home. Before we left, I told them that in my mind, what had happened was over. This day was a new day and we were a new team. Their slate was clean, but no more shenanigans would be tolerated. Only time would tell if I had handled it right.

When I got home I shared the experience with my wife and she was tremendously supportive. Once again we turned to the only thing we knew we could trust. We agreed and stood on Romans

8:28 "and we know that all things work together for good to them that love God, to them who are the called according to his purpose." I trusted God. I didn't know why He allowed this to happen, but He can take the work of the enemy and turn it into good. It was in His hands. Hebrews 11:1 rang in my ears. "Now faith is the substance of things hoped for, the evidence of things not seen."

God had not brought me to London to dessert me.

WORKERS FOR
THE HARVEST

Romans 4:21 "and being fully persuaded that what he had
promised, he was able also to perform."

There was a great deal of work to be done. Even though our first football game was only 10 weeks away, our varsity coaching staff still was not complete. It isn't possible to over-estimate the importance of a good staff. As I have mentioned earlier, I had a good staff my first year at London, but we were never able to work together. I take full responsibility for what happened. First impressions are lasting and even though we tried to make it work, we just couldn't work through our differences.

Several coaches of our feeder programs remained intact, although none were on the teaching staff. Our freshmen football coaches, Ron Gibson, David Mans, Scott McKinney and Jon Thomas remained intact. Our Junior High program was coached by Richard Cunningham, Doug Huff, and John Lickliter. All but

John Lickliter had been involved in the system the year before. Jon Thomas was the only one who was not a Red Raider alumnus. It was a great group of men assigned to handle the lower-level programs. I had given a great deal of consideration to moving a couple of these men to the varsity level, but after much thought and prayer, I decided that they could best serve us where they were. Because of the instability of the coaching staff, I felt that in the long run, we would be better off if we did not have to rob Peter to pay Paul. I knew that all of these men would be loyal to our program. Maybe they did not know me well enough to commit to me, but they were loyal to London High School. Our school administrators did anticipate several teaching openings, and it was our hope to be able to fill them with quality teachers who could also coach.

One piece of good news had arrived earlier in the spring. Norm Emmets, former head football coach at London and currently our softball coach, had shared with me that after a 2 year lay-off he felt he was ready to get back into football. I had known Norm for about 15 years going back to when he had been a very successful coach at Centerburg and Fredericktown High Schools. My assignment at London was teaching learning disabled students, and in this situation, Norm and I team-taught troubled youngsters. It did not take very long for both of us to realize that we thought a lot alike. I had always had a great deal of respect for Coach Emmets, but I really began to appreciate him when I saw how concerned he was for kids.

Norm was a gentle giant. At 6'1", 260 pounds, his large frame was topped off by a full head of sandy-blonde hair sitting atop a light-complexioned, oval face. Norm's ever-present prescription eyeglasses changed colors with the light. His booming voice could be clearly heard down the narrow halls or across the flat practice fields of London High School. His intensity was inspiring, and his "get it done whatever it takes" attitude was refreshing.

A graduate of Findlay College in northwest Ohio, Norm was originally from New Jersey, and his wife, Barb, is a physical therapist at a Columbus hospital. He is a devoted family man who gives all that he has to his sons Jacob, 8, and Jon, 4. Although in his early 40s, his positive energy made him seem much younger.

Long ago I learned that you cannot fool kids. It doesn't matter so much what you say, but it matters a great deal what you do. It was obvious from the start that this man cared about others. Norm went out of his way to support programs and kids that had no bearing on him at London. If there was an FFA banquet, he was there. If the choir had a concert, he was there. If a group needed help, he was there. I knew he was the kind of person that I wanted to work with.

Norm had been the head football coach at London for 2 seasons before I arrived. He was only beginning to make progress in rebuilding the program when he also began to have problems within his staff. When his staff fell apart and he could get no assurances that he could bring in new coaches, Norm chose to resign. He had coached for 2 years as an assistant at Capital University, a small liberal arts college in Columbus, when London called and asked him to return as a teacher. He accepted and had been back at London one year when I arrived.

We never discussed the reasons that lead to him originally leaving London. I know that he was very highly thought of by the administration, and that they had not wanted him to resign. I had watched him closely over the past year and knew that we would make a great partnership. . I was convinced that getting him was just what we needed and that God was preparing the way for me by moving Norm Emmets back to London. Returning to coach at London would be a difficult move for him to make, requiring him to take a step down from the position he had once occupied. If he would be willing to take a step down and help, it would speak volumes about his character.

Football coaches are for the most part very egotistical, self-centered people. I believe that is the nature of the position. Coaches are always under the microscope and every action is second guessed and criticized by people who have no idea of the intricacies involved with running a program. In order to survive in this business you have to be able to shrug off all of the criticism. A strong belief in yourself and your system is a must. In order for Coach Emmets to agree to help restore our football program, he was going to have to be willing to humble himself. If he had chosen not to resign when he did, I was sure that he would still have been head football coach at London, and the program would have enjoyed success. Would he now be willing to come back and help someone else do that job?

Right or wrong, the head coach gets most of the credit and blame, and if we were successful, Norm would be helping to make me look good. Norm understood the roles each person played on a team. I believe that he knew that no coach at London could be successful if he had to work alone. Although he never said it, I sensed that he felt that he had left the job undone and that his return to London would enable him to see the job completed. He wasn't worried about the opinions of others. Matthew 23:12 says "And whoever exalts himself shall be abased; and he that shall humble himself shall be exalted." To my delight, he agreed to become our defensive coordinator. That was the day our program began to turn around.

There was only one member of the coaching staff from the previous year who still remained. Doug Moshier was a young man who had served as a quasi-coach, but was actually an athletic trainer. He was the type of young man who would do anything that was asked of him. Even though Doug came in with the staff that preceded me he had remained loyal throughout the previous season. I know that there were many times that he had been caught in the middle, but he had the best interests of our football program at heart. We cleared the air during the off season and I knew that I could count on Doug.

Doug is a 30 year old graduate of Wilmington College. At 5'10", 230 pounds, "Coach Mo" had dropped about 40 pounds in the previous couple of years. He was a thickly built, blond haired, blue eyed, dedicated educator. Doug's wife, Jody, teaches horticulture at Westerville City Schools in northern Columbus.

There was one problem with Coach Moshier. He really wasn't a coach. He would be willing to work in whatever capacity we asked him to, but his greatest strength was that he was a fine athletic trainer. I wanted him to do that full time and not be burdened with coaching responsibilities. A good trainer is worth his weight in gold. We agreed that Doug would be with us for the 1990 season and we would worry about the capacity later. His loyalty was a big plus.

Although I believe that our coaching staff was assembled by God, it was not done without a great deal of faith in the face of multitudes of obstacles. The addition of Mark Collier to the London staff did more to increase my faith than anything that had ever happened before.

Mark had been the quarterback of my first Heath team in 1981. He was always the type of young man that you would want your son to be like. He played for me for three years at Heath and then went to my alma mater, Otterbein College. He gave up his senior year of eligibility at Otterbein and became a member of our coaching staff at Heath. At one time he had considered going into the ministry, but God led him down another path. He graduated from Otterbein and took a job teaching math and coaching at Springfield Northwestern. Now at age 24, he was completing his second year of teaching.

Mark was a thickly built 5'10", 200-pounder with thinning, sandy-brown hair. He was enthusiastic and demonstrative and focused on his desire to improve the quality of life for the kids that he worked with.

Mark was the consummate coach, scheduling his wedding on a weekend before the football season began, so that he would not have to miss practice. He was married on a Saturday and began two-a-day practices on Monday. His wife, Chris, a student at Wright State University in Dayton, is still waiting for their honeymoon.

When I took the job at London, the first person that I thought of was Mark. It appeared that we were going to have a math opening at London and I contacted Mark about coming with me. The job ended up not materializing, but I shared with Mark that God had told me that he would be on my coaching staff. A year later, God would fulfill that prophecy.

Two of the coaches from our previous staff were math teachers and they had made it very clear that they had no intentions of remaining at London in 1990. In April, I contacted Mark again and he agreed to come to London. After he interviewed with our superintendent, Dr. Jacob Froning, I was assured that when a math position became available he would be offered a job. It all seemed to be falling into place. I was in London to do God's work and He was providing workers to aid in the harvest. I should have known that Satan would not let loose without a fight. He mounted an attack so strong that without a strong faith in God, I might have given up the battle.

In late June, one of our math teachers announced to all of us that he had a job. He was returning to his home area as a math teacher and assistant football coach. His desire had been to return home, so it seemed like God's hand must be involved. Mark and I were in Dr. Froning's office when a call came from the coach's new employer. They were simply doing a reference check and informed Dr. Froning that he was their top candidate and that he would be recommended to the Board for hiring on July 11. However, there were complications. Ohio State law requires a school to release a teacher from a contract prior to July 10. After that date, a teacher is bound to the school to which he is already under contract. The school where Mark was currently employed had a history of adhering strictly to that date. It didn't appear that the job would be open in time for Mark to resign his old position. Dr. Froning called the administration at Northwestern and explained the situation. They agreed to release Mark from his contract as long as it happened on the 11. It appeared that the problem had been solved and that Mark was on his way to joining our staff. I told Mark that I would call him from Dr. Froning's office when we received word that our other coach had resigned.

We looked happily toward that day and began planning his move to London. Unfortunately, we were not out of the woods.

On July 11, I arrived at Dr. Froning's office to see if our math teacher had resigned. He said that he hadn't and decided to call the school and see if he had been offered a contract. As Dr. Froning spoke on the phone with their principal, I could almost hear Satan laughing. It seemed as though one of the members of their School Board had a teacher that he wanted to see in the math position. Even though the administration had recommended our coach for the position, someone else had gotten the job. I don't know when I have ever felt so discouraged in my life. We had no position for Mark.

So many times in my life when things didn't turn out the way I wanted, I had either blamed God for going back on his promise, or written it off as not being what God had planned for me. I knew better now. I knew that Satan was behind all of this and that according to the Word, God's answers are only "yes" and "Amen." I called Mark, and broke the bad news to him. I told him that God had promised me that he was coming to London and that I knew God would not let me down. I agreed to call him back in a few hours after I had time to think.

I went to the Bible. That always seems to be a good place to turn when I am confused. I had spent some time reminding God of the promises that he had made to me and that I knew he was not going to go back on His word. The situation seemed impossible, and I have found that is when God does His best work. I opened up my Bible and found myself in Romans 4. My eyes zoomed onto the 21st verse, which I had highlighted in red sometime before as I was reading. There it was! God was speaking to me as plainly as He could. Chills ran down my spine as God confirmed His word to me. "Yet with the respect to the promise of God, he did not waver in unbelief, but grew strong in faith, giving glory to God, and being fully persuaded that what He had promised, He was able also to perform." I scurried to the phone and called Mark. I shared with him what I had just read and we agreed over the phone that we were going to stand together on God's promise to us. I knew in my heart that it was done.

There still was no position for Mark; at least not in the natural realm, but we both knew it was just a matter of time. Although there appeared to be no possibilities on the horizon, we knew God was in control. Mark told me that in a few days he had something that he wanted to share with me but that the time was not yet right. I could tell that he had received the same confirmation that I had received because he was unshakable in his faith. So convinced was he, that he resigned his job in Springfield, signed a lease on an apartment in London, and made plans to move. The only teaching position that we had was eighth grade science, and Mark was not certified to teach that. Whenever someone asked him what he was teaching, he always replied "Math. I just don't know where yet." Two days before football practice was to begin, our answer arrived.

Coach Emmets, Coach Collier, Coach Moshier, and I were standing around after football conditioning talking about how we could get Mark a job. You know how people are, always trying to help God out. I mentioned that the only opening was science, and that position had been filled at the board meeting the previous night. Coach Moshier commented that was too bad because Mr. Brake, a high school math teacher, was certified K-8 and could teach science. My spirit jumped in anticipation.

The first thing the next morning I was in Dr. Froning's office and I found him sitting alone at his desk. He offered me a chair and we exchanged pleasantries. I immediately got to the point.

"Dr. Froning, I am really concerned about this situation with Mark Collier. He has stood with me in great faith about coming to London and I was just checking to see if there wasn't something that we could do."

He looked at me sincerely through his gray-rimmed glasses.

"Yes," he said, "I've been thinking what a shame it would be to lose that fine young man. It's just that our hands are tied until somebody resigns."

"Did we fill that eighth grade science position last night?" I asked. I knew plans had been made to employ someone at the board meeting the previous night.

"No we didn't," he replied. "For some reason, I didn't feel right about doing it last night, so we held off until the August meeting."

I took in a deep breath and spoke boldly. "Did you know, Dr. Froning, that Mr. Brake is certified to teach Science? His certification is K-8. If he could be transferred to that position, then that would open a math job somewhere in the district for Mark. I know that is a lot to ask, but he is really valuable in our attempt to move forward. He'd be a real asset to our program both as a coach and a teacher."

I paused to read his reaction. As he sat in his black pinstriped suit, I searched his countenance for a sign of uneasiness. As he raised his large hand to stroke his face, he never batted an eye.

"I never thought about that," he said. "I think we can do that. I'll start the paperwork today. I know that not everyone will be happy with this decision, but we have to get you some help. When you talk to Mark, tell him of our plans and I will notify his principal that we intend to offer Mark a contract."

We shook hands, and he wished me luck. I hit the door running and praising the Lord. God works on His own timetable. When the time was right, He made the way. Just that quickly, it was over. I am convinced that God has a sense of humor, and in my mind's eye, I can see Him in His make-believe scoreboard clock countdown. "Five.four.three." as He throws in the last second winning shot over Satan. I could almost see the victory dance in Heaven.

The next day when Mark and I got together I asked him to share with me what it was that he had been unable to tell me earlier. I knew that God had His hand in the matter, but what Mark shared with me that day was almost beyond imagination. It all goes back to the evening when we found out that his job had not come through.

After we spoke briefly that night, I said that I would call him back when I had gathered my thoughts. As I turned to the Bible for my strength, Mark Collier, forty-five miles away, was sitting in his apartment reading through a Guideposts magazine. He didn't even know where it had come from because he did not subscribe to it. Somehow it had found its way into his house. He was reading a story in it and eventually began to lose interest. As he was thumbing through it, he came to a short story in the back. He quickly read it and was struck by the Bible verse quoted at the end. It was Romans 4:21. As he placed the Guideposts down on the table in front of him, he knew that God was not finished yet. Within minutes his phone rang, and he picked it up only to hear me on the other end sharing with him the promise of Romans 4:21! Is it any wonder that we both knew it would work out in the end?

God had brought us a long way. Just a few short months earlier, I was a football coach without a staff. Within the last two weeks, He had filled in the missing pieces.

Brian Shirley was a 30-year-old young man who was changing careers. He had just recently completed his training at Wright State University in biology. As fate would have it, one of our biology teachers resigned late in the summer and we just happened upon Coach Shirley. Although he had played sports, he had never coached football before. I liked him immediately. He was enthusiastic, willing to learn, and a mature first year teacher. We were lucky to get him and he got better each day as he became more comfortable with the system. At 5'9", 165 pounds, he was athletic looking. His dark black hair and black mustache made him look distinguished and gave him instant credibility with the kids. My only concern was that as a young father of two, he would not understand the time commitment necessary to be a successful coach.

The day before practice began, God plugged in the missing piece. Mark Byard was a graduate of Capital University looking for his first teaching job. He was an English teacher, and English teachers who can coach are a rare breed. Coach Byard had played

4 years of football at Capital. One of his coaches had been Norm Emmets. I was immediately struck by his happy-go-lucky, optimistic attitude. His youthful enthusiasm and willingness to contribute was just what we needed. In his physical appearance, Mark resembled me. At 5'9", 200 pounds, he was larger than I, but we shared the same stocky body build. In a lot of ways he reminded me of myself 15 years ago. The same message came through in all of his references. He was a quality young man with an ultra positive attitude, who did not look at the problem, but rather, for the solution. We were ready to begin work.

Every time I look back on the events of the summer, I am overcome with an awesome respect for the power of God. It would be so easy to write all of the events off as coincidence. In fact, many people still do. I know that this coaching staff was handpicked by God and no one will ever convince me otherwise.

I think our greatest mistake as Christians is that we give up too quickly on God. We are the McDonald's generation. "I want my hamburger, and I don't want to have to wait on it." Somewhere we have lost the ability to trust and to wait. At the first sign of trouble, we want to hang our head and give up, thinking God has not heard our feeble prayer.

Could it be that we really do not know God? If we were to see Him for who He really is, we would never doubt His ability and desire to work in our lives. He is our Father. Oh, if we could somehow get the revelation of what that means! Matthew 7:9 "Or what man is there of you, whom if his son ask bread, will give him a stone? Or if he ask a fish, will he give him a serpent? If ye then, being evil, know how to give good gifts to your children, how much more shall your Father which is in Heaven give good things to them that ask him?" Think about that a minute. Let it sink in. What wouldn't you do for your son?

The problem is not God; it is us. If we truly knew Him, His true nature, we would realize that His love provides all that we need.

God's assembling of our staff was a miracle, but it was just the beginning of the work that lay ahead.

RENEWING YOUR MIND

*Romans 12:1 " I beseech you therefore, brethren, by the
mercies of God, that you present your bodies a living sacrifice,
holy, acceptable unto God, which is your reasonable service.
And be not conformed to this world, but be ye transformed by
the renewing of your mind, that you may prove what is that
good, and acceptable, and perfect, will of God."*

Now that the coaching staff was in place, we could begin the task of molding this group of young men into a family unit. It would be a formidable task. In order to create the type of cohesiveness that we were looking for from our players, it would be necessary for our coaching staff to bond into a close-knit group. Not only did the coaches not know each other very well, the coaches and players did not know each other at all. Coach Moshier and I were the only ones who really knew the kids, and our player-coach relationship was shaky at best. As the old saying goes, we had a long way to go and a short time to get there.

Our staff hit it off immediately. Coach Emmets and I had a

confidence in each other and our relationship was solid. Coach Collier knew me and our system and loyalty was never in question. Coach Shirley and Coach Byard were both hard workers and happy just to be with us. Coach Moshier and the freshmen coaches had been around for a year and were more confident in our system. The big thing was that we liked each other. We were friends. That made practice fun.

We were still faced with two big problems. None of the coaches knew who the kids were and vice-versa. That made it very difficult to try to evaluate talent and placement of players. Until the coaches could get to know the strengths and weaknesses of each player, it was very hard to discuss personnel. As head coach I had many ideas about who belonged where but a good coaching staff will use input from everyone to make the decisions. Many times one coach may see something in a young man that no one else could see. The fact that so many faces were new was something that I hoped would work to our advantage in the long run. With an entirely new staff every kid got a fresh start. There were no preconceived ideas or opinions about the abilities or attitudes of the players. I cautioned the returning coaches to keep all opinions to themselves so that we would be able to fairly evaluate each athlete.

The second problem was one of learning our system. Although football is football, and there are only so many ways to do something, each system has its own terminology. Our goal was to try to make sure that each of our coaches knew what to teach before he went onto the field. At times, the coaches were only one day ahead of the players. The willingness of our coaches to learn and take advice showed that they were all very secure in who they were and what they could offer to our program. Our guidelines were simple: Treat the young men as you would want your son to be treated, and don't be afraid to coach. I promised each coach that I would never correct him on the field, and that he needed to let the athletes know that he was in charge of his designated group. It was important that each coach knew that I was not watching over his shoulder, and I promised that I would never ask them to teach something that they didn't feel competent to teach.

I was struck immediately by the enthusiasm. Our coaches dove into their jobs, and the practice field became a whirlwind of activity. Daily, a new attitude was being created at London High School. I sensed the change, and I knew that the kids did too. It wasn't something that you could put a finger on, but the winds of change were blowing.

Many times programs that are struggling will look for excuses as to why they are not being successful. It is not uncommon to hear people blame everything from players to facilities. It is easy to do, and helps us justify why things are not going well.

Our facilities at London were not very good, and it would have been easy to use them as an excuse. London High School is a modest, relatively new facility that was built in 1980. It took eight different elections before the community finally approved the bond levy to build it, and with each levy failure the size of the building shrunk. It is a nice school, but many of the things that most schools have were eliminated because of an increase in construction costs.

Our practice facility was very poor. Ten years after the school was built, nothing had been done in the way of landscaping to make the fields around the school usable. The only flat area on the entire school grounds was the front lawn of the school. This was where our practice field was located. It hurts the appearance of the school to have a front lawn that has been trampled brown by the repeated thundering of athletes during the hot summer months. It is punctuated by one thin set of goal posts, put there as if to explain why the lawn looks so barren. All of the other area is made up of large mounds of dirt that still remain from the construction. The school district owns about fifty acres behind the school that they one day hope to develop, but even as of now, it is of no use at all.

With the exception of the mounds of dirt, our school was surrounded by flat farm fields. In the summer and fall they are alive with the corn that the farmers have planted, and the corn serves as a good shield against the constantly blowing winds that sweep across the flat farmland. After the harvest in the fall, the area takes on a desolate look, as the only thing visible in the fields is the stubble of the previous year's corn crop. Off to the west lies the ominous view of Madison County Correctional Institution, our maximum security, state-of-the-art prison facility. Its high fences and constantly burning security lights are an ever present reminder of what lack of education can do for you.

If at all possible, our game field was even worse. All of our home games were played at vonKannel field, which is located in the heart of downtown London. The new school was built on farmland on the northern outskirts of town, but the game field has remained in the same place where London has played football since they first fielded a team in the early 1900's. The distance from the high school to vonKannel is two miles, and on game days, all of our equipment had to be moved downtown. The field itself is something right out of the movies.

High Street is the main drag in town, and it borders vonKannel field on the north. The field sits so close to the street that any time an extra point is kicked at the north end of the field, the football ends up out in the street. It was not unusual for the ball to be run over by a car or to have someone stop and pick up the ball and drive away.

The east side of the field is bordered by Shaw Elevator. This is one of the places where the local farmers buy and sell their grain. Shaw's has several large concrete grain bins which tower above the lights of the field. There is also a railroad that runs by Shaw's and it is not unusual for a locomotive to come roaring through town less than 100 yards from the field, while the quarterback is barking out the signals, trying to drive his team down the field.

Sitting just outside the southeast corner of the field is Dial Corporation. This is the factory where all of the world's Brillo Pads are made. The proximity of the soap factory causes the air to be permeated by the constant smell of soap that seems to hang in the air like a cloud. On some of Ohio's hot, humid, breezeless nights, the smell can become very thick. Many opponents have complained about the great home field advantage created by the roar of the trains and the smell of the soap.

The other two sides of the field are bordered by another set of railroad tracks to the south, and a small creek that runs the length of the field on the east. On the far side of the creek stands the Dixie Drive-in. The Dixie is a favorite stop on Saturday mornings for all of those who want to discuss Friday night's game over a hot cup of coffee. Every decision is chewed over by some of London's most loyal fans, and it is not uncommon to have the Coach be the main entrée on the morning breakfast plate.

The playing surface itself is adequate enough unless you are bothered by the fact that our high school baseball field bumps up against the east corner of the field. During baseball season, it is important that you have an agile centerfielder because it will be necessary for him to chase fly balls and avoid the football light poles that stand in the middle of the outfield.

Our locker facility at the field is probably the worst in the state of Ohio. Actually, "locker room" is a misnomer because there is not one locker on the entire premises. The facility is really two garages stuck together with public restroom facilities in the middle. The old red and white cement block building has no heat and poor ventilation. In the winter it is cold and in the summer it is sweltering. There is one toilet to service everyone on the team, so the players learn to go to the restroom before they come to the field. Pre-game jitters can cause a back-up at the toilet as players stand in line waiting to relieve a nervous bladder. The only light fixtures are a series of bulbs that hang from the ceiling much the same as you would find in the basement of an older home. There are no showers and no hooks upon which to hang your clothes. It is, pure and simple, a garage that doubles as a locker room.

The most unique feature of the field is that those who arrive early have the opportunity to park their cars ringside.literally. Although there are bleachers on both sides of the field, the east and south ends of the fields double as parking lots. Many folks arrive early enough to get the prime parking spots, pulling their cars up against the restraining wire encircling the field. Some sit on top of the hoods of their cars enjoying a ring-side seat less than 30 feet from the fierce action on the field. This unique feature gives one the feeling that they are watching an old-fashioned drive-in movie, enjoying the up-close action from the safety of their car. A great play on the field results in a cacophony of honking horns from the cars snuggled up against the field

It would have been easy to use the facilities as an excuse, but we constantly harped on the positives: the uniqueness of our field and the tremendous home-field advantage that it gives us.

In between practices we tried to do positive things with the kids. Often one of the coaches would share a story or an experience from his life and we would develop a thought for the day. I knew that these life-lessons had a positive effect because it was not unusual for a player to reference a comment that someone had made weeks before.

One of the thoughts was "when all is said and done, more is usually said than done." We talked about how some people talk a good game and yet contribute nothing at all. It is far more important to contribute with one's actions, rather than only with one's mouth.

The slogan that I had chosen for this year's football team was COUNT ON ME. This slogan was put on our shirts and hung in our locker room. This addressed exactly what I saw as our biggest problem. We needed to convince these kids that they had to rely on each other to accomplish our goals. It was hard enough to beat the opponent without having to worry about the commitment of the man beside you.

One evening as I was lying in my waterbed reading from the Word, I came across Romans 12 and that verse penetrated into my spirit. That was it! Renew your mind. I couldn't wait until the next morning.

The next morning, at the beginning of practice, I gathered the football team together and I quoted to them that verse from

Romans. For the next 10 minutes, the Spirit of the Lord ministered to the dry souls of a group of young men who were hungering for a vision.

"Don't you guys see how this relates to us? We have got to change the way that we think. God has uniquely created each of us with individual talents and abilities. We are the greatest of all of His creations, yet we allow ourselves to be beat down by the opinions and attitudes of those around us. So much of what we think and believe is dictated to us by others. Your parents and friends will tell you that there is no way that you will ever be able to beat West Jefferson, planting seeds of doubt and unbelief in you. Whether you know it or not, once those seeds of doubt are planted in your mind, it is very hard to overcome. Gradually, the thoughts and opinions of others begin to take root and grow in your mind, and you are defeated before the game is ever played."

"Can anybody explain to me why West Jefferson should have a better football team than we do?"

A warm, dry breeze was blowing, causing a rustling in the corn fields, as I paused to wait for a response.

"Do you mean to tell me that just because someone happens to live in a town ten miles from here that they are going to be a better football player than you? That doesn't even make sense. West Jefferson is successful because they expect to be successful. They have a different way of thinking about themselves.

"What in the world does last year's football team have to do with this year's? Just because we lost last year does not mean we have to lose this year. If you want things to change, then you are going to have to change. You're going to have to change the way that you think. That is what we are trying to get you to see. Renew your mind. Change your way of thinking. Get rid of "stinkin thinkin". If we concentrate on the negative aspect, then negative things are going to happen. We have so many great things going for us. All we have to do is begin to focus on those."

It was as quiet as I can ever remember it being outside. The Holy Spirit was speaking through me and the message was being received. I asked the offensive linemen to stand.

"Kenny, Aundrey, Ben, Seth, Aaron, stand up."

They rose nervously to their feet. I pointed at them and spoke to the team.

"Can you guys tell me any team that we will play that will have a better front line than these five guys? West Jeff? Academy? Big Nut? Who is going to be able to top these guys?

"The problem is that we don't look at it that way. We look at all of the weak areas.at all of the things that we can't do, and we waste so much energy worrying about them. Well, no more! We are renewing our minds. We're changing the way that we think. I know that we can be great, but it doesn't matter what I know, it matters what you know. You have got to convince yourself that you are something special and then begin to look for all the things that you have to offer. Once we focus in on that, we will be able to see that God truly wants us to be successful."

A car in need of a muffler sped down the highway with some teenagers hanging out the windows honking its horn, breaking the silence of the morning. No one seemed to notice.

"You see, guys, we spend so much time listening to the lies that other people tell us. You hear your classmates say that you are going to get beat and you believe them. Your parents say the coaches don't know what they are doing and you believe them and slowly the strength of our team is sapped away because of what somebody else thinks. What in the world do your classmates know about our football team? What do your parents know? Do they attend our practices? Are they experts in coaching? No, they're not. But because they have an opinion, we allow them to affect the way that we think. They are slowly stealing from you. Not on purpose, but every time you listen to what they say about our team, you lessen the chances that we will be successful. Don't listen to them! You know the truth.you're here every day. You know what goes on. Renew your mind. Think good thoughts. Expect great things to happen."

To end the meeting, I asked several players to stand and say something nice about one of their teammates. It was great to hear some of the comments that the players had to say about each other. There was a great deal of respect and admiration for each other. As they spoke, you could see the pride come over the individual players. Most of them had no idea that one of their buddies thought that highly of them. The public affirmation that the players received from their teammates became the building blocks of a new foundation.

"I think that you guys realize that we've got a lot going for us. Let's concentrate on those things. We can be as great as we want to be. If you can believe it, you can achieve it. Listen to the last part of this verse, 'Prove what the will of God is, that which is good, acceptable and perfect.' That's what God wants for us. Let's do our best to get it."

Practice usually lasted about two hours and was very demanding in the hot August sun. Our kids gave us great effort that morning. As we left the field, Coach Emmets walked up to me.

"Coach, that was awesome," he said, his round face beaming.

"Yes, they worked hard today," I replied as I felt the beads of sweat run down my back.

"I'm not talking about how they worked. I'm talking about what happened out there. I don't know just what it was, but something changed today," he said.

I felt it too, but I thought that maybe I was the only one. On that hot August afternoon, God had sent fresh oil from Heaven. A bond was beginning to form and a seed had been planted. It was up to us to continue to water the message, but I knew it had taken root. I knew we had the chance to be a good team, but only if we could change our thinking and win the battle of the mind. As we walked off the field, I had a sense that something great was happening. Dry bones were beginning to come to life!

UNASHAMED

Romans 1:16 "For I am not ashamed of the gospel of Christ: for it is the power of God unto Salvation to ever one that believeth,"

I had been forewarned by a number of people what a difficult and demanding town that London was for a coach. Because of the success that London had experienced in the past, many of the supporters in town could not understand why the program had fallen on such hard times. The community wanted a winning team in the worst way, yet they were afraid to put a great deal of hope into this new football season and this new coach for fear that they would be disappointed again.

Our hopes were high as we headed into the new season, but we were still fighting a lot of negative aspects in town. We had just completed a great two-a-day session and had been successful in getting the young men to focus toward team goals rather than individual accomplishments. Even though things had gone relatively well in our scrimmages, the real test of our team would come when we were faced with adversity. We had asked several young men to change positions and the attitude had been one of cooperation. As long as things were going well, it would be easy to be a team player. It was imperative that we get off to a good start to maintain the confidence of our players.

The first game of the season would be against our next door neighbor, Madison Plains. On any year, this was a very emotional game, but this year it was even more so because of some off-the-field changes that had occurred. We were unsure just how the kids would react.

Madison Plains was operating under a completely new coaching staff, which in most years would be a real advantage for us. However, this set of circumstances was a little different. The coaching staff at Madison Plains was essentially the same staff that had coached at London the year before I arrived. Our ex-athletic director had taken the football job at Plains and he had taken two of the members of my previous staff with him. This made for a potentially volatile situation. Many of our kids were bitter at their old coaches, feeling that they had been betrayed by un-fulfilled promises. I knew that our players did not understand the reasons why the coaches had left, but many of them had developed a close relationship with those men. We were now asking our players to switch their loyalties and to trust our coaching staff. I didn't know what to expect.

I also had some strong personal feelings about the game. Not only did I want to win the game so that we would get off to a good start, but I felt that my credibility was on the line. It would be a lie to say that I did not harbor some ill feelings towards some of the coaches at Madison Plains. I also felt a sense of betrayal because of some of the treatment I had received. Motives are important, and I wanted to be sure that my energies were directed towards winning for the right reason.

During the week of the game we had tried not to let the game become a battle of coaches. As I said before, the kids had strong feelings of their own. We did mention that the Madison Plains staff knew them well and that they would try to capitalize on their weaknesses. We tried to share with them the importance of the game for our own honor.

Personally, I had to fight my own feelings. Even though I knew that the Lord had removed those men from London, I still harbored some bitterness about the treatment I had received the year before. I knew Hebrews 10:30 well, "Vengeance belongeth unto me," and I fought those feelings all week. I truly wanted to get on with the season, and I wanted my motives to be pure before the Lord. I knew He could not reward me if there was bitterness in my heart.

That is the great thing about a personal relationship with Jesus Christ. I am not sure that I, in my flesh, could have let go of those feelings. My pride had been hurt and I was resentful. If I expected the players to renew their minds and change the way they thought, I had to be willing to do the same. I turned it over to the Lord. I confessed to Him that I had tried to let go of my feelings, but that I was having trouble. I knew that I could not do it on my own, but that through Christ, all things are possible. I repented, put it in the Lord's hand, and moved forward.

On Thursday night before the game I was reading my Bible when God directed me to Matthew 5:23. "Therefore if thou bring thy gift to the altar, and there rememberest that thy brother hath ought against thee;" I knew that scripture was for me.

As we took the field before the game on this warm, clear, August night, there was an air of excitement in the crowd. The visitor's bleachers were filled with green and gold dressed fans as they stared across the field at the mass of red and white that filled up the home sideline. As the players ran through their pre-game drills, I was led to the opposite end of the field. I went to each of the Madison Plains coaches, shook their hands, and told them that I had no hard feelings. I'm not sure whether or not they considered me a hypocrite, but I do know that at that moment Christ relieved me of that burden. It had not been easy to do. It was comforting to know that I was responsible for my own actions, and not for how they responded to them.

We defeated the Golden Eagles 21-0 in a hard-fought, clean football game. Before we left the field that night, we gathered for the Lord's Prayer as we always did. At the conclusion of the prayer, I spoke to the team.

"We are so proud of you guys. You played with a lot of class in the midst of what we all know was a tough week."

Players had arms draped over each other's shoulders, and tears were freely flowing as I looked into their trusting eyes.

"We can be great," I continued, "but only if you guys are willing to commit to me. I can't change what has happened in the past; I can only tell you about the future.

Listen closely: I'm not going anywhere. I'm going to be football coach at London for a long time. My family is here. My kids are in this school. I have committed to this community, but this relationship will not work unless you are willing to put your trust in me. I know what we can become, and I know that I can lead us there, but you are going to have to forget all of the times that you have been lied to in the past. This is a new season. All things have become new. We have got to lean on each other and work together as we move forward."

Some looked at me through their red helmets, others had mud stained faces, but all eyes were full of hope and promise.

"I love you guys. Great things lie ahead of us. All we have to do is go and get it. Let's give it all that we've got."

As we left the field it was great to know that the pressure of that game was over. It had been quite a week.

Pastor Ron Grant at the London First Church of God had contacted me earlier in the summer about organizing a day where his congregation could honor our team. Pastor Grant had a son on the team, so he had a particular interest in our football program. We had settled on August 26, the Sunday after the Madison Plains game, as the day for the service.

All of the football players and their families had been invited to attend. We had encouraged our players to come, but there really wasn't anything that we could do to force them to come. It was our hope that we would be able to get some people to attend church who normally would not have been there. I was pleased to arrive that morning to find over half of our players and parents had come.

The First Church of God is a cozy little country church situated two miles south of town. It sits back about two hundred feet off of the main highway and is surrounded on two sides by corn fields. The sanctuary is small with a seating capacity of about two hundred, and it was filled on this bright sunny morning. The small altar is elevated about four feet in the front of the sanctuary. On this warm morning, the windows were open to allow the fresh, cool breeze of the morning to blow freely, causing the drapes in the windows to sway. The sound of birds singing and an occasional passing car presented a solemn background to the service.

Mark Collier and I had both agreed to speak and share our testimony with those in attendance. Mark was eloquent and inspiring as he spoke first, sharing the events that had lead up to his arrival in London. He spoke of how our faith, working together, had made it possible for him to be a part of this coaching staff. I know that our players saw a different side of him that day.

I looked forward with anticipation to my opportunity to share my story with the congregation. I had not made any plans about what I was going to say, but rather, prayed that the Holy Spirit would anoint me with a message.

I believe that I understand our constitution and the co-called separation of church and state, but I do not think that our founding fathers ever meant for our schools to be void of the mention of God. The Constitution states that congress shall make no laws regarding the establishment of religion. I fail to see how talking about God in schools can be construed as an establishment of religion. We go to great measures to educate the mental and physical aspects of our students but, by law, we are not even permitted to mention the spiritual dimension of man. We assume that the churches will take care of that for us. This idea is great except for the fact that many families never go to church and, as a result, receive no spiritual instruction at all. As an educator, I understand the importance of spiritual training and I know that a great number of our students do not receive any at all. I honestly believe that the answer for many of the problems in our schools can be traced to the fact that so many kids have no clear set of morals or values. As Christians, we have been forced to keep our beliefs in the closet. Like it or not, kids pattern themselves after certain models. I want to be that model for kids, and I want so much to be able to share with them why I am the way that I am. Unfortunately, our courts will say that is not legal. It is frustrating to not be able to share with them what has worked in my own life. If I knew a better way to lose weight, everyone would want me to share it with them, but if I shared a better way to live their lives, I would be preaching. Why can't I share both and allow them to make their own decisions?

God really spoke through me that day. Because I was in church I was able to finally open up and share with our team the calling that God had made upon my life. I spoke about how I had ended up in London, the same story I have written about in this book. The tears flowed freely down my face as I shared with the congregation the miracles that God had performed in my life. I unashamedly bared my soul and God used that moment to demonstrate the commitment that I had to London High School. It is one thing to be committed because I coach there. It is something else to be committed because God put me there.

I know that our players saw me differently from that day forward. They could no longer question my sincerity toward them and they knew that I was there to stay.

That public confession of faith opened up other avenues as well. The attitudes many parents had towards me changed when they realized that I was a Christian. Several parents shared with me that they had been praying for a Christian coach for London High School. The fact that I was in London was an example of God working in more than one life at a time. As I walked out of church that day, for the first time, London was beginning to feel like home.

Spiritual Warfare

*Ephesians 6:12 "For we wrestle not against flesh and blood,
but against principalities, against powers, against the rulers of
the darkness of this world, against spiritual wickedness in
high [places]."*

I t was a relief to have that first victory under our belts. It seemed
as though we had lived forever under the pressure of Madison
Plains. Finally, with that victory securely tucked away, we could get
on with the rest of the season.

Our second opponent of the season was Circleville High School.
Circleville is a town that is very similar to London in that it is the
county seat of Pickaway County. It was established as an agricultural hub for that county because so many of the residents had at
one time been involved in some aspect of agriculture. The town
was named after a famous Indian burial ground that was located
in Pickaway County. This particular Indian tribe had built burial
mounds in a circle, and the town of Circleville had developed in
the midst of them. Thus the name Circleville, "Roundtown," as

many people call it, is located forty-five miles southeast of London. Like London, it sits in the middle of miles and miles of farm fields used for all types of grain. Although Circleville is only twenty minutes south of Columbus, it had not yet experienced the growth that many other small towns on the outskirts of the city had gone through. Circleville's old, established downtown area with rows of brick buildings, town square, and courthouse, hold a striking resemblance to London. It was a strong reminder of days past when football games consisted of one small town playing another. With the advent of the suburbs, much of this tradition has passed.

The Tiger football team had mirrored London in recent years. The past was full of great teams and accomplishments, but it had been over a decade since Circleville had experienced any degree of football success. They had hired a new coach in their attempt to return to the glory days.

They had been beaten badly in their first game of the season. My old Heath team had blasted them 45-6. This lopsided loss caused us a great deal of concern. When you play someone after a lopsided loss a couple of different things can happen.

The first thing is that a team tends to come back from a loss like that with a vengeance. If they have any pride at all, they will want to prove to their fans that they are better than they have shown. I knew that Circleville believed that they could beat us, and they would have the advantage of a large home crowd on their side.

Our second concern was that we would have an emotional letdown from the Plains game. We had pointed toward that game for a long time and it is only natural to relax after a big win. I knew that our kids would not take Circleville seriously, and we fought that attitude all week long. Unfortunately, we were never able to get them focused on the task at hand.

Many of us have a misconception of God. We don't realize that He is concerned about the everyday affairs of our lives. He wants us to succeed and do well. For years, I believed that it was wrong to bother God about such trivial matters, but I have since realized that He is omniscient, all knowing, and He is aware of them anyway. To pray for victory seemed wrong because I would be asking God to choose sides. The Bible convinced me that I was wrong.

God wants great things for us. He wants us to be successful. Deuteronomy 28 teaches about the blessings that God has in store for us. And it shall come to pass, if thou shalt hearken diligently unto the voice of the LORD thy God, to observe and to do all his commandments which I command thee this day, that the LORD thy God will set thee on high above all nations of the earth: And all these blessings shall come on thee, and overtake thee, if thou shalt hearken unto the voice of the LORD thy God." God's blessings are for me because I know that I am in God's will. However, in order to claim them, I am going to have to deal with many forces, including the power of Satan.

As I have talked about earlier, I believe that Satan is the most misunderstood of all of God's creations. He works constantly in our lives and is able to convince us that it is all God's doing. John 10:10 says, "The thief cometh not, but for to steal, and to kill, and to destroy: I am come that they might have life, and that they might have it more abundantly." The thief is Satan. What does he want to steal? I believe that he is after the blessings that God has in store for me. I know that football is only a game, but it is what God has called me to do. Satan wants to destroy it. The whole purpose for God sending His Son was to give us victory over all of the devices of the devil. God realized that Satan had such control on our lives that we would never be able to fellowship with Him in the manner that God wanted us to. To break that bondage and re-establish our relationship, God sacrificed His only Son as payment for our sins. I John 3:8 says "He that committeth sin is of the devil; for the devil sinneth from the beginning. For this purpose the Son of God was manifested, that he might destroy the works of the devil. Jesus came to destroy Satan's work in our lives, the stealing and killing and destructive things that he does. God has done all that He will ever do. Christ's death and resurrection have given us power over the enemy. If we fail to use it, we certainly can't lay the blame at the feet of God.

We scored in the second quarter against Circleville, after a long, well-sustained drive. We made that lead stand up until late in the fourth quarter. The Tigers then began to mount a serious challenge. Our defense had played well the entire game, but the Black and Red began to punch holes into our defense. Although the momentum was swinging, I knew that this game was ours for the taking. God had promised us victory. The thief was trying to rob it from us.

Earlier in my life I might have offered up a prayer to God to help us in the game, but now I realized the power that we had through Jesus Christ. I wasn't going to sit around and beg God to help. I was going to fight for what I knew belonged to me.

Late in the fourth quarter, Circleville, moving from right to left, was nearing our goal line. For the entire game, we had been able to hold them off, but now they were playing inspired ball and sensed that they could win the game. Our kids were getting flustered and were beginning to point the finger at each other on the field.

I slipped the head phones off and slowly walked toward the opposite end of our bench. I bent down and filled a Gatorade cup full of water out of the yellow cooler and continued away from the action. I stopped, looked into the sky, and began to declare aloud, "Lord I know that you did not bring me here to fail. You have promised us in your Word that we would be the head and not the tail; above and not beneath, that the victory belonged to us. Father, I claim this victory in the name of your Son, Jesus Christ. Satan, I rebuke you. You and all of your spirits and any weapon that you would form against us are bound up in the name of Jesus Christ of Nazareth, and by the power of that Name, I command you to go from us now. You have no power or authority here. Thank you, Jesus, for the victory and for the great things that I know you are going to do through me and through this team. In Jesus' name, Amen."

This whole battle had taken a matter of seconds, but I knew

that victory had been secured. In faith, I returned to our football team.

The Red and Black continued their assault against our end zone. With twenty seconds left in the game, they were faced with a fourth down and goal from our 16 yard line. Circleville called time out and Coach Emmets jogged out on the field to talk to the defense.

The contrast in the two huddles was visible. The Tigers were excited and enthusiastic as they listened to the last minute instructions of their coach. Our huddle was quiet and worried as Coach Emmets tried to rally them for this last big play.

In recent years, both of these teams had seen the breaks go against them in the latter part of the game. It was hard for our kids to believe in themselves when they had been disappointed so many times before.

As the coaches ran off of the field, the players lined up for one more play. Circleville's quarterback dropped back and looked over the middle. Breaking from the left side was a black-clad receiver. While our defensive backs settled into their zones, this receiver wove his way in between the white jerseys and pulled in the pass as he slid along the turf into the end zone. The score was 7-6.

Circleville lined up for the game tying kick. I continued to pray as I bent over with my hands on my knees. I looked across the field to see the Tigers' coach, backed by a sea of black uniforms, assuming the same posture as I.

My eyes flashed back to the 22 players near the end zone. If the kick was good, we would play overtime to determine the winner. If it missed, we would emerge victorious by the skin of our teeth.

The kicker and holder lined up seven yards deep. For a moment, all movement seemed to stop as all players waited for the snap. When the ball was snapped, black jerseys and white jerseys pushed against each other in an effort to protect or block the kick. I followed the flight of the snap. It was a bit high and to the left and the holder had to reach across the tee to catch it. That small movement destroyed the timing of the kicker and he made a stutter-step as he waited for the ball to be placed down. The ball fluttered high in the air and sailed off into the dark night, wide of the goal posts. Victory was secure.

We didn't win the game because God was on our side or because He wanted us to win more than Circleville. We won because I knew who was trying to steal this game away from us, and I didn't stand by and allow him to do it.

We were lucky to come out of the game with a 7-6 victory. We had played about as poorly on offense as any team of mine ever had. The Tigers had played inspired ball and really deserved to win the game. I know that we won the game because of a battle that took place in another arena, one that could not be seen.

To the unbeliever, this may seem nuts, but I can only share with you what I have seen work in my life. Not all spiritual battles are that easy. In fact, most are long and difficult to wage. On this night I had caught the enemy off guard and secured what the Lord had promised belonged to us.

My life has changed since I have become aware of Satan's desire to destroy my life. I take authority over him every day and try not to give him any entryway into my life. He is persistent and he is subtle, but I know who he is.

Is my life easier because of it? I don't really think it is. But I know that the weapons that Satan uses against me will work only if I fail to fight back. The victory has already been granted to me, but I am going to have to be willing to fight the battle. On the cross, Christ cried, "It is finished." He meant that His purpose for coming, to destroy the works of the devil, was completed. His part of the battle is over. He didn't say that we wouldn't have any battles.only that victory would be ours. That victory is ours through the name of Jesus Christ.

Praise God, for the first time in 13 years, London was 2-0!

BLESSED THROUGH
PERSECUTION

Matthew 5:11 "Blessed are ye when men shall revile you, and persecute you and say all manner of evil against you falsely, for my sake."

Although we had won our first two consecutive football games of any given season for the first time since 1977, the coaching staff still did not have a real good feel for our team. We had played very inconsistently and were not nearly the team that we had hoped we would be.

As long as the team is winning, there is a real tendency on the part of the fans to think that everything is going well. As coaches, it is our job to make an honest appraisal of our progress to determine what areas need improvement. Even after victories, it is important to not lose sight of our weaknesses and pay a price for that later. You can be sure that your next opponent is studying you, searching for weaknesses.

Although we had won both games, we knew that we had a long way to go before we became a good football team. It was apparent that we had the talent, but we had not plugged all of the pieces into the proper slots. Our team identity was still evolving and this made it difficult to identify just what we did best. We knew that some moves needed to be made, but we were hesitant to make the changes without giving the individuals ample time to prove themselves. It was important to give the machine a chance to work before we looked for new parts.

Unfortunately, the schedule did not afford us the luxury of waiting too long. Our next two games were against West Jefferson and Columbus Academy, two of the best teams on our schedule. Both schools were perennial league and state powers, and we had to play them back to back. Going into the season we knew that this would be a critical point in our schedule, but if we were going to have a good season, we felt that we needed to win at least one of the games. We had our work cut out for us.

West Jefferson had been beaten the previous week by Licking Valley. West Jeff was not used to losing to anyone, and we knew that they would be looking to vent their frustrations on somebody. This was supposed to be a down year for them, but there was a lot of pride and tradition in that program, and they were not about to go quietly into the night.

West Jefferson is a town ten miles east of London that sits on the outer edge of Columbus. They have a great football tradition having won over eighty-five percent of their games in the decade of the 80's. It is different than London in that football is the focus of its entire athletic program. Although they offer other programs, the Roughriders prided themselves on having great football teams.

This did not sit well with the fans in London. They did not enjoy losing to the Brown and Gold. During London's football heyday, West Jeff would not play us. Only in the previous seven years since our program had begun to flounder had West Jeff put us back on the schedule. We had not beaten them in recent memory. To many of our fans, West Jefferson was the measure of success. If we did not beat them, then the rest of the schedule was meaningless. The London-West Jeff game was the battle for Madison County.

Our kids had a good week of preparation, but we were a team that hoped to win, while they were a team that expected to win. London had not been in a big game like this in a long time, and we wanted our kids to be loose and ready to play. We were confident as we went into the game because West Jefferson had trouble moving the ball the first two weeks of the season. Everything pointed toward a low scoring, hard-hitting football game.

West Jefferson scored on their first possession, and you could just see their confidence rise. Our offensive problems from the week before continued, and we watched them jump out to a 28-0 halftime score.

We were very disheartened as we entered our locker room. The heat in the poorly ventilated garage was unbearable and forced us to sit out in the open air, where the soap laden air filled our lungs. We had allowed them to get the momentum and were unable to get it back. The coaches were encouraged because it was obvious that our kids were playing as hard as they could. We made some adjustments and asked them to continue playing hard, knowing good things would eventually happen.

West Jefferson ended up beating us 34-14, but we played a good second half. We felt that there was definitely something for us to build on, but we knew that Academy would be every bit as tough as West Jeff.

There is no teacher like experience. As we reviewed the films of the game we realized that our kids had not played within themselves. Because it was such an important game, our kids had tried to do more than they could. Rather than each man doing his job, the players tried to go the extra mile. This caused the kids to get away from their individual techniques. We had played hard, but we had not played smart. We played the second half more within ourselves and looked more like a team. I know that the kids were sky high for the game, but because they were not used to being in a big game situation, they did not know how to respond. Sometimes a loss can be a good thing if you learn from it, and I think we left that game a much better team.

After viewing the films, I was even more convinced that changes needed to be made. It was the consensus of the coaching staff that we had the best players on the field, but we did not have everyone in the proper places. In my mind, there was no reason why we should be struggling so much on offense. Something needed to be done to stir things up. The moves were subtle, but their purpose was to make us a more balanced offensive unit.

We took our best receiver and moved him from tight end to wide receiver. Curtis Skoot was a 6'4", 200 pound junior with large soft hands attached to long arms. His black face was characterized by large expressive eyes and a warm smile. We needed to get the ball to him more and had not been successful with him at tight end. As a side note, Curtis had only agreed to play football as a sophomore because I beat him in a one- on-one basketball game. He wasn't going to play football because he wanted to dedicate himself totally to basketball, so one morning in the city park; I challenged him to a game of one-on-one. If I won, he played football. If Curtis won, he didn't. Final score: 5' 7" Coach, 8... 6'4"Curtis, 3.

To fill his slot at tight end, we inserted Chad Teeler. Chad was not a very good receiver, but was potentially a more consistent blocker. Chad was thickly muscled but inexperienced because he had not played the year before. Three games into his senior season it was now time to find out if he would be able to help us.

Another move was to shift our offensive linemen around. We interchanged Ben Stronger, a guard, and Aundrey Clapper, a tackle, to better utilize their strengths. One of Academy's defensive linemen was considered the best in the league and we put Aundrey over him because he was our best drive blocker. We hoped that he would be able to help contain him.

Aundrey had a story of his own. He had come to football camp twenty pounds overweight, and summer practice had been very difficult for him. His attitude had faded to the point where one afternoon he quit the team. Later that evening he had second thoughts and came by to ask me to accept his apology. After talking for about an hour, I finally told him that if he was serious, then he would have to put up or shut up. He owed our team six miles and payment must come the next morning. I made plans to pick him up at 7:00a.m.when we would drive him six miles outside of town and let him run in to practice. Only then would we reconsider his status.

I awakened at 6:00 a.m. to a drenching thunderstorm. What should I do? Would it be too cruel to ask him to run in the rain? As I picked up Coach Collier, I asked what he thought about making Aundrey run.

"I think he is going to get his butt wet," was his curt reply.

As we pulled up to his door, it was all I could do to keep from laughing. Out of the house stepped Aundrey with a trash bag pulled over his massive body to keep him dry. His hat was tugged down over his head and he had on his best Ninja Turtle look.

"Does your grandma know what you are going to do?" I asked him.

"Yeah," was his matter-of-fact reply.

"What does she think about it?" I asked.

"She thinks I better do what you say." He replied.

We drove outside of town and dropped him off in the middle of a big downpour and then questioned our compassion all the way to school.

An hour and ten minutes later he came running down the drive. His teammates cheered him, and from that day on, he became a more committed player.

The final move was to begin using a sophomore as one of our tailbacks. Dwight Johnson was a 5'7, 135 pound speedster. Although he physically was not ready to handle the job full time, we knew that he had the skills necessary to be a fine player. We were looking for a spark and hoped that he would provide it. Dwight had rushed for over seventy yards in the fourth quarter of the West

Jeff game, and we hoped that his added speed would give us another dimension. The combination of his speed mixed with the power of Jason Smakers gave a strong combination at tail-back.

Whenever you make changes in the middle of the season, you run the risk of disrupting the chemistry of your team. The kids think the moves are necessary because you don't have confidence in them. We were able to convince them that the reasons behind the moves were designed to make us a better team in the long run.

It was a calculated risk on our part, but we knew that the team on the field the first three weeks of the season would not be successful against the schedule we had to play. The moves were sound, and they were subtle, but only time would tell if we had done the right thing.

Columbus Academy is a private school located on the east side of Columbus. Twice during the decade of the 80's they had won the Division IV state football championship. They were always a very good football team and not one that other teams looked forward to playing. The Central Buckeye League was breaking up after this season, and many people pointed the finger directly at Academy. Because of their ability to draw students from all over the Midwest, they are able to be very selective when structuring a football team. Many of the small public schools have resented having to play them because they usually delivered a shellacking to you. In fact, two years before this, they were ahead of London 40-0 at halftime when a severe thunderstorm hit, and the game was never finished. The previous coach made the decision not to return the next day to finish the game. It was a horrible message to send to the team. Quitting should never be an option. To say the least, battling Academy would be a monumental task.

Friday morning dawned rainy and windy, just what we did not need to unveil our new offensive look. As the day progressed the rain subsided, but the wind would be a factor all day long. The wind always blows across the flat lands of Madison County, but that day the wind was especially strong. Our home field advantage was somewhat alleviated by the fact that the wind was blowing toward Dial, rather than away from it. We could not count on our soap cloud this night.

We scored first against Academy on a forty-eight yard trap up the middle to our fullback, Mike Fishman. We turned the ball over twice in the second quarter and as a result, only ran thirteen offensive plays the whole first half. Late in the first half the Maroon and Gray fell on a fumble at our 35 yard line. Six plays later the Vikings scored to take a 7-6 halftime lead. We had played well against a good team and were confident going into the second half.

We had the ball first to begin the second half, and found ourselves driving right to left into the teeth of a stiff wind. On a third and nineteen, I was foolish enough to try to pass the ball into the wind. The pass seemed to stop at its peak and flutter into the outstretched arms of the enemy at our forty yard line. I should have known better. The result was to give them the football in great field position with the wind to their backs. They were able to drive the ball in from there for a 14-6 lead. We played conservatively the rest of the quarter, hoping to move the ball when we got the wind. Our defense was stellar, and as the quarter changed, we were in great position to pull the game out.

Twice during the fourth quarter, we were able to drive the length of the field only to stall deep in Academy's territory. Once we were held fourth-and-one on the eleven yard line as Fishman was stopped on a straight ahead plunge into a mass of humanity. On our next possession, we drove the ball deep into their territory again. The scoreboard clock had ticked to less than two minutes, and time was at a premium. I called for a pass to Curtis in the back of the end zone.

Our QB, Joe, retreated three steps and lofted a tight spiral into the right back corner of the end zone. At 6'4", Curtis towered over the defender who was draped tightly against his back. Curtis extended his arms and reached for the ball only to see it slip through his hands like a bar of Dial soap.

After a trap to Fishman netted two yards, I called again for another pass to Skoots. I had confidence in him that he would catch it and I wanted him to know that we were not afraid to go to him again. As the clock ticked to less than one minute, Joe took the snap and rolled quickly to his right. On his fifth step, he set his feet and delivered the ball to the receiver. From my vantage point on the sideline, I could sense that the pass had been thrown with perfect timing. My eyes quickly jumped down field to pick up Curtis. I focused in just in time to see him slip to the turf as he made his cut to the sidelines. The excitement quickly evaporated as the ball stuck like a dart in the left arm of Academy's defensive back. Academy took one snap, fell on the ball, and the game was over. I knew that we had come up one play short against a great team.

Both Academy and West Jefferson would go on to 8-2 football seasons.

I was proud of our football team. They had shown great courage in the two fourth quarter drives. I was encouraged as we left the field. To fans it was another loss. I saw it differently. For the first time in weeks I liked what I saw on the field.

As a team we always gathered together on the field after the game. We talked about the game and began to point toward the next week. Before we broke up, we said the Lord's Prayer and left the field as a group.

Waiting to meet the team as we left the field were our fans. Many offered encouragement and condolences as we passed toward the locker room. In the middle of the crowd was a man who did not appreciate me as a coach. He yelled to all of the players as they passed him.

"Good job. Keep playing hard. We'll be okay as soon as we get a coach."

Over and over he repeated those statements. Our assistant coaches were irate. As we stood against our locker room door two of them had to be restrained from going over and confronting this man. One coach was in tears because he knew that I poured my heart and soul into our team, and it hurt him to see someone trying to destroy what we had spent months building. It was not easy, but I asked all the coaches not to respond.

I was reminded of Christ. I thought of Him as he hung on the cross and cried, "Forgive them, Father, for they know not what they do." I didn't need to defend myself to this man. He didn't know what he was talking about, and I wasn't going to give any credence to what he said. I answered to God and to the London School Board, and I knew that I had their support.

As we walked down High Street to the school, two of the seniors came up to me and put their arms around me.

"Don't pay any attention to him, Coach," Kenny said. "We know you know what you're doing."

"Don't let them run you out of town the way they have all the other coaches. We need you to stay. You're the man who can turn this place around," said an emotional Ben Stronger.

Tears welled up in my eyes and I swallowed to control the lump in my throat.

"Don't worry about me. I'm not going anywhere. I've got a job to do. It will take more than that guy to get me out of here," I said as I slapped them on the back.

As we walked arm and arm over the railroad tracks, past the grain elevator toward the school, I couldn't help but think back to that June camp-out. The same boys who were afraid to trust me were now stepping forward to defend me. I knew that God was with me, and I could sense something special going on around us. I was confident in His plans.

I couldn't wait to see what would happen next.

Diggin' Holes,
Plantin' Poles, and
Stringin' Wire

I Corinthians 12:14 "
For the body is not one member, but many."

Homecoming weekend was on the horizon. Our next opponent was to be Grandview Heights in our annual homecoming game. Grandview was a game that we felt we should win, but it would be necessary for us to rally the troops after two disappointing losses in a row.

Grandview is the smallest school in our league. It is a small, older, established community near the heart of downtown Columbus. A land-locked community, its expansion was stunted by the growth of Columbus around it, and now it found itself with no room to expand. It was a proud white-collar community with a high mixture of different ethnic groups. It is also my wife's hometown, which gave the game special meaning in the Daubenmire house.

It was our custom to bring the football players in on Saturday mornings after the Friday night game to review films and check for injuries. It was also a good time to put the previous game behind us and begin preparation for our next opponent.

I was pleased with the attitude that I saw on that morning.

Although we had lost the football game there were a lot of positive things that had happened. The changes that we had made for the game had worked out well. As we watched the film, it was obvious that we should have won the game. If we had made a few key plays at critical times, we would have come out on top.

I didn't have to convince the players that we were a good team. They could see it on film. Of course our confidence was down, but the players were determined to have a successful season, and were encouraged with the way we played against such a powerful opponent.

It was always my nature to be positive, and I always tried to conclude our team meetings on an upbeat note. This particular morning I felt it was necessary for the players to hear from each other. To finish up our meeting, I called on each of the seniors to give his own impression about where we were and where we were headed. One by one, they shared their thoughts, and all seemed to agree that we needed to stay together and work harder. The last boy I called on was Zach Korns.

"Zach, what do you think?"

I'll never forget what he did or what he said. Zach stood slowly to his feet from near the top row of the bleachers that we were occupying in the gym. He looked at me, and then slowly eyeballed his teammates, who were scattered about this small section of bleachers, and then looked back at me. Shuffling his feet and tilting his head back confidently, he cast the vision.

"Fellas," he declared, "I think we ought to go 8-2."

I felt as if a bubble had burst inside my heart. That was a

thought that was almost too wild to think about. A London team going 8-2! That meant we would have to win our last six games. Most people would have laughed. In fact, no one spoke. Somehow in their silence, a spirit of agreement was at work, and these young men were convinced that they could do it.

Homecoming provided just the hype that we needed that week. School spirit was up as it always is homecoming week, and our kids worked hard. The coaches were very conscious of the need to build the team up in an attempt to instill some of the confidence that we had lost. It was a crucial game, and the players knew it. The student body helped out by wearing red and white to school each day during the week.

My family and I always try to go to church on Wednesday night. We always enjoy it, but it can be quite a hassle getting ready to go. That Wednesday night, I got home late from practice. Michele was in a cheerful mood and had the kids ready for church. I told her that I didn't really feel like going.

"That's why you should go. You know you'll get blessed," she said.

I ate quickly and then piled into our 1987 Dodge Caravan for the forty minute trip to church. On this particular night, I just wanted to stay home and rest, but I headed to church anyway.

Thank God for a good wife. I'd hate to think how the year might have been different had I not gone that night. God knew what He was doing when He brought me and Michele together. We are the perfect match in that we are never in a down mood at the same time. We are always able to pick each other up and say the right thing at the right time. She was just what I needed that night.

There was no doubt that this was the biggest week of the season for us. We had just come through two games against the toughest opponents we would play all year, and now we were going to play two teams that we felt we really should beat. If we were to lose either of the next two games, it would be very difficult for us to have a good season. From any standpoint, a 6-4 season would be considered a success. Without victories the next two weeks, that goal might slip out of reach.

My life had changed ever since I started to attend World Harvest Church. Always before, I had gone to church because I felt that I should; now I went to church because I wanted to. The place was alive. All you had to do was spend one service in that church and you could no longer doubt that God was real. Every service was uplifting, inspiring, and spontaneous. I don't know how I had faced the problems of this world without a personal relationship with Christ. World Harvest Church introduced Him to me and my life was transformed.

Something had tried very hard to keep me out of church that night. My head was filled with all of the reasons why I shouldn't go. I have come to realize that Satan is a liar and the father of lies and that we should do the opposite of what he tells us. If he tells us to stay home, then we should go. The key is being able to hear the "small, still voice" which is the prodding of the Holy Spirit. We miss out on the blessings of God because we listen to the great deceiver.

On this Wednesday night, Ted Walters, an assistant pastor at World Harvest, delivered the message. Most people are disappointed when someone other than Pastor Parsley gives the message because he is such an anointed preacher. This evening it was obvious that God had chosen a different vessel to work through.

He shared a powerful message on how God's work is not always glamorous. God never said that it would be. In fact, He promised us just the opposite. John 16:33 "These things I have spoken unto you, that in me ye might have peace. In the world ye shall have tribulation: but be of good cheer; I have overcome the world." He has promised us trouble, but He has also promised us victory. Being a Christian is more than jumping and shouting. It involves faith, and strength, and overcoming. It is a battle that must be fought daily. Those who follow Christ should not expect a road without bumps, but rather a life full of problems that can be overcome through the power of Christ.

Christians should be different from other people. Our attitudes about life and our purpose here should help light the paths of our neighbors. If we who are filled with the Holy Spirit act no differently than the average person, then our testimony of Christ is useless. It is not that we do not have problems; it is that we have the answer to them. If we go around complaining and bellyaching, then we deny the power of Christ in our lives. How can we hope to win others?

As I left church that night I knew that God had prepared my game plan for Friday night. Ted Walters shared a story that night that would become the theme for our football team during this important week.

Before every home football game, our team dressed at the old high school which is located downtown. We arrived early to tape injuries and walk through our plays on the gymnasium floor. It was an opportunity to get together early and begin focusing on the task at hand. Before we walked to the field that night, I called the team together, and with some embellishment of my own, shared the story that Ted Walters had given me two nights before.

"Fellas, gather up. I'd like to share something with you. It is a story that I think really represents our football team. It is the nature of our game that the guys who run and catch the ball are the ones who get their names in the paper. The guys in the trenches, making the blocks, are responsible for the success or failure of our team. Everyone in this room knows that.

"This story is about a man who worked for the Ohio Power Company. For forty years, he went to work every day, in all types of weather. He didn't say much and hardly any of his co-workers knew much about him. Whenever someone brought up the subject of work, his response was always the same. "I'm just diggin' holes, plantin' poles, and stringin' wire." He never complained or second-guessed, but instead went about his business the best he could. 'Diggin' holes, plantin' poles, stringin' wire' was the way he greeted his co-workers in the morning and the way he left them each night. For forty years he had been at this job and his attitude had never changed. No one could figure him out."

As I looked around the room at the players dressed in their red jerseys and white pants, all eyes were focused on me. Often during this pre-game meeting they were fidgety and inattentive, but not this night. All eyes bore in on mine.

"Finally the day arrived that he should retire from his job, and all of his coworkers planned a surprise party for him on his final day. As they presented him with his gifts, one of the employees said that he had always wanted to know what he meant when he talked about diggin' holes, plantin' poles, and stringin' wires. The group grew quiet as the old man's bright blue eyes lit up. As the old man's crooked fingers stroked his weathered face, and he removed his hat exposing his thinning white hair, he spoke softly.

"For forty years I've come to this job, and I've seen a lot of people come and go. I have been able to stay here so long because I realized a long time ago the importance of what I was doing. It is sort of like doing God's work. We can't all be the preacher. Someone has to sweep the sanctuary and clean the toilets. Over the years I came up with the saying 'diggin' holes, plantin' poles, and stringin' wire.' It is that thought that kept me going during the longest of days. To you young fellers, this job may seem dull and meaningless, but that is only because you don't see the big picture. You don't understand the importance of what you do and how you connect to the bigger picture. Next Friday night, boys, down in Cincinnati, they are going to open up Riverfront Stadium. Over 55,000 people are going to show up to watch the Reds play. They are coming to watch Pete Rose, Johnny Bench, and Joe Morgan, but I know that without me, there wouldn't be no game. You see, some man in Cincinnati is going to go over and push a button, and that great stadium is going to light up bright as day. 55,000 screaming fans are going to come to their feet, and history will be made. Now they won't call out my name, and they won't put my picture up on the scoreboard, but I want you to know that I'll be feeling pretty good as I sit on my porch and listen to the game on my old transistor radio. Maybe nobody knows it besides me and

God, but there wouldn't be no game if it hadn't been for me diggin' holes, plantin' poles, and stringin' wire!'

As I paused I could see the impact of the story on the faces of the young men before me. I looked into black faces and white faces. I saw eyes filled with confidence and others with fear. But in every face I saw confirmation that they understood what I had said. It had hit home.

"That's us guys. We've all got a job to do. The Bible talks about being one body, but yet very separate parts. Without each one of us doing what he is supposed to do, the body does not function properly. But when we all work together for a common goal, we become an unstoppable force. As we walk to the field this evening, through the heart of this town that you so proudly represent, focus on the miles and miles of electric wire that line the road. Look at the lights in the stores and the clock on top of the courthouse. We don't know who is responsible for it, but because of him, all of London has power. Tonight, when every player does his job, we are going to use the power that those wires provide, and we are going to light up our scoreboard. Do your job, don't worry about your buddy, and we will be rewarded."

Sometimes you know when a message has hit home. This one was a bull's-eye.

I followed behind our players as we walked to the gridiron and I could feel them bond. They looked at the wires and talked quietly among themselves as we flowed like a red river toward the field. Something invisibly-powerful had happened.

We jumped out to an early lead but allowed the Bobcats a miracle score on the last play of the first half. This gave Grandview a great deal of momentum and put them right back into the game. We had some breakdowns in the second half, and as we entered the fourth quarter we were behind 19-18.

We had the ball to begin the fourth quarter and we needed to re-establish our momentum. We began a drive that quickly took us deep into Grandview's territory. The Bobcats called timeout, and I ran onto the field to talk to our offense.

"Great job, guys. How are we doing?" I asked as I looked into the sweat and mud-marred faces of those young warriors with steam escaping from the ear-holes in their helmets

"Coach, we're just diggin' holes, and plantin' poles," blurted out one of our linemen.

I looked into Aundrey's face for some sign of doubt or fatigue. Our eyes met and his bright, black, ninja-face beamed with confidence.

"Yeah. Just keep handing it off, and we'll all meet in the end zone," he said as he looked around at his buddies. As I gave final instructions, all eleven players joined hands and I turned and left the huddle. As I jogged off the field, I knew that we would win the game.

Two plays later, Mike Fishman slammed off tackle into the end zone, and another score on our next possession sealed the 30-19 homecoming victory. As the game ended, we were on the fifteen yard line driving for a third fourth-quarter score. When the game was on the line, we responded. Every man did his job, and Grandview could not stop our assault. For the first time, we believed in ourselves and in each other. We were becoming a team.

When we left the field, our band was there to meet us. The London Police closed down High Street, and as the band played, we all marched the half mile back to the middle school. It was beyond belief. Months before people had warned me against walking to and from the field. They were afraid that we would be spit on and mocked. As the eternal optimist, I had predicted that just the opposite would happen; it would turn into a victory march. Now, here was the entire downtown of London put on hold while their conquering heroes marched through.

After the game, our local sports reporter Dina Pierce was interviewing some of our offensive linemen because they had been so dominant. What a switch. She wasn't talking to the quarterback or the running back, but rather, to the men in the trenches.

"In that fourth quarter, you guys were really moving them off the line," she said. "What was the difference?"

"We were doing what Coach told us to do," came the reply, "Just diggin' holes, plantin' poles, and stringin' wire."

POWER OF THE TONGUE

Proverbs 13:3 "He that keepeth his mouth keepeth his life:
but he that openeth wide his lips shall have destruction."

We were, at that point, half-way through our football season. Our record was 32, which was not bad, but in order for us to have a winning record, we would have to duplicate that the second half of the season. That would not be easy. We would soon be moving into divisional play within our conference, and to win three of those games would take a great effort. We had hoped to be 4-1 at the midway point but had lost one of the games we thought we should win. The good news was that we were a team on the rise. We had gotten better the past three weeks, and we knew we'd have to continue to improve.

Our next game was against Jonathan Alder. It would be the last inner divisional conference game. Academy, Grandview and Alder were all in our league, but they were not in our division. Even though, the games all counted toward the league standings. If we were to defeat Alder, we would be 2-1 against the other division, which would help us when it came to determining the league champion.

Jonathan Alder was the last of three Madison County schools that we played. It is located in the town of Plain City which is in the northernmost part of the county. The school was named after an earlier American explorer and bore the nickname Pioneers.

Jonathan Alder was a team that caused us a great deal of concern. They were 1-4 coming into our game and were also operating under a new coach. During the previous year, we played them at their home turf, and we had performed like we were in a mental fog. We fell behind 20-0 at halftime only to stage a furious fourth quarter rally that came up short 20-18. We scored all of our points in the fourth quarter, but had waited too long to start playing. At the end of the game, it was obvious that we were the better team, but they had the victory. It had been a crucial game in our season, and we had fallen flat on our faces. We never recovered from it. Alder had used that game as a springboard to a fine 7-3 season.

Due to a quirk in the schedule, we had to play at Jonathan Alder for the second year in a row. I know that I harbored bad memories from the game the year before, and I was not very excited to return to the scene of the crime. We talked all week about the importance of being ready to play and reminded the players of what had happened the year before. The Grandview game the week before had been an emotional victory, and I was afraid we would not be able to forget about it.

On this Friday, we played the same type of game against the Pioneers as we had the year before. We were lethargic and unfocused, and Alder was fired up and ready to play. We drove seventy yards to score in the final minute of the first half to tie the game at halftime 14-14. We were lucky that we weren't behind.

It was one of those hot muggy nights that are so common in Ohio in the fall. A thick haze seemed to hover over the field, so thick that you could actually see the rays of light as they passed onto the field. Because of the heat, we could not go into the locker room at half-time, but instead gathered the players around us in one corner of the parking lot near the school. As the players leaned against the yellow school buses that had transported us to the game, we got on the kids pretty hard and challenged them to go out and play the second half up to our potential. It has been my experience that once you are in the middle of the battle, it is awfully hard to change your attitude. If you are lethargic the first half, chances are that same type of attitude will persist the rest of the game.

I believe that it was a sign of our rapidly-developing maturity that we were able to pull ourselves together and win the game 20-14. Our defense became much more consistent and our offensive line took control as we ground out the victory.

At halftime of the game I finally came to the realization that I had made a grievous error during the week of preparation. I am always very careful to control what I say. I have always understood the power of my words upon those I work with. By the simple utterances of my mouth, I can build up or tear down, calm or anger, heal or hurt. What I have not always understood is the prophetic powers of our tongue upon our future.

A word once spoken can never be retracted. The sound of those words will reverberate around in the spiritual realm forever. That is why the Bible says "That every idle word that men shall speak, they shall give account thereof in the day of judgment." (Matthew 12:36) God has given us the ability to speak. If we are Born-again, Spirit- filled believers, then what we say is backed up by God. He does not want us to use this powerful instrument carelessly.

It is a common phrase to hear someone say that he spoke without thinking. In all actuality, that is impossible. What is a thought? Where does it originate? Does a thought come from outside the mind and then enter in, or is it in there all the time waiting to be brought out? I'm not sure that I know the answer. Man is three dimensional. He is body, mind and spirit. It seems to me that outside forces control what we think in our mind. Let me try to explain.

As you sit here reading this book your mind is at work gathering information. If someone in the other room were to begin popping corn the aroma may make you hungry. Without the outside stimulus of the smell, you may never have even thought about popcorn. The smell initiated the thought. The thought of eating that popcorn then comes in contact with your physical body, which may result in your stomach growling. The decision as to whether or not you will eat any corn will then be a conscious decision made by your heart. Do you have the power to choose whether or not to eat the corn? Of course you do. We call that will-power. I'm sure we've all heard Matthew 26:41 "the spirit indeed is willing, but the flesh is weak."

One of the entryways of Satan into our lives is through our thoughts. Because of the thoughts that the enemy has planted in our heads, many of us are defeated before we ever begin. Negative thoughts enter our mind, we believe them, and as a result, we become powerless over it. I used to laugh at the cartoons where the devil would sit on a man's shoulder and tell him to do something wrong, while at the same time an angel sat on the other shoulder and shook his head "no". I'm not so sure that that isn't really how it happens. God is not going to stop Satan from tempting you, but he has given you the power to choose what is right. James 4:7 says "Submit yourselves therefore to God. Resist the devil and he will flee from you." The devil's greatest attacks are in the mind.

There is nothing wrong with having bad thoughts. That is the nature of man. What becomes sinful is to dwell on those thoughts or to act upon them. God tells us to resist them, and they will go away. Proverbs 4:23 says "Keep thy heart with all diligence; for out of it are the issues of life." Don't allow those evil, negative thoughts to take root. If you allow your spirit to control your mind and don't allow your mind to control your spirit, then you will not speak in a careless manner.

During the week leading up to the Jonathan Alder game, I had been listening to some of those lies of Satan. He was constantly reminding me of how poorly we had played last year and how I could not rely on how our kids would perform. The more I concentrated on those negative thoughts, the more fearful I became about the upcoming game. I was losing the battleground of the mind.

Faith and fear are two mutually exclusive things. It is not possible for them to abide at the same time in the same heart. Where there is fear, there is no faith, and where there is faith, there is no fear. I bought the lie that Satan was trying to sell me. The least I could have done was to keep my big mouth shut and not spread those negative thoughts to others.

That, of course, is easier said than done. All week long at practice, I cautioned the kids about their attitudes. Because I was constantly reminding myself about last year, I thought it was necessary for me to remind the kids. I shared my fear with them that I wasn't concerned about how Jonathan Alder was going to play, but that I was very concerned about how we would play. I used great sayings like these:

"If we play like we did last year, we're going to be in a battle."

"I'm afraid that you guys are going to take them lightly."

"We better not go up there and sleep through the first half like we did last year."

I was lucky that I never mentioned getting beaten, or I believe that too would have manifested itself in our football camp.

I spent the week planting the seeds of fear and doubt and that is exactly the crop that we reaped on Friday. We played with fear, and doubt, and as if we were asleep.

Someone, somewhere, must have been interceding for us because we were able to pull the victory out.

It was a cheap lesson. I know what power I have through Jesus Christ, and I will be careful to not exalt the thoughts of the enemy above what I know is God's will for my life.

Satan works on us enough. How could I be foolish enough to invite him in? "Renew your mind, stupid! Get rid of stinkin', thinkin'!" I said to myself. Thank God we were 4-2!

To God Be the Glory

Luke 17:17-18 And Jesus answering said, Were there not ten cleansed? but where are the nine? There are not found that returned to give glory to God, save this stranger."

I have often wondered how God could love man. We are so fickle. When things are going well, everyone wants to be a part of the group. As soon as things turn sour, we are quick to abandon ship. Nowhere is this better illustrated than in the world of athletics.

After two straight victories, our team was beginning to come together. Because of our recent success, our attitude was great, and the kids were really buying into what we were trying to do. After we had lost back-to-back games earlier in the year, some of the players began to point fingers, trying to figure out why we were having problems. Winning usually puts a stop to that.

After sixteen years of coaching, I have come to realize that a coach is only as good as his last game. It is reality that we are judged by the performance of a group of teenage boys on a Friday night. If the team doesn't win, then that week has been a failure. A victory does not allow much time to celebrate. We have to immediately begin preparing for the next game. In pursuit of victories, I really believe that we have lost sight of the role of the high school football coach. Just what was my job?

The goal of any coach is to win as many football games as possible, but should that be the sole focus? Should coaches ignore the academic, social, and spiritual development of our players? If a coach is judged on wins and losses, then it becomes very tempting to sacrifice what we know is right in order to win a game. I have tried my whole career to judge my performance by a different measuring stick. I believe that my job is to turn out as many fine people as I can. Even though others will say that they share the same goal, ultimately, a coach will keep his job only if the "W's" out-number the "L's".

Even as a high school athlete, I understood the impact that a coach can have on a young man's life. I have not taken that responsibility lightly. The biggest mistake a coach can make is to compromise his values in order to please a person or a group. In my previous ten years as a head football coach, my teams had never had better than a 5-5 record. We accomplished that four different times while I was at Heath, but we were never able to be a big winner. Yet, I am convinced that I am a good coach. Webster's Dictionary defines coach as "one who instructs or trains a performer or team." I have done that, and not at the expense of winning games. Our players leave us as better people. The sad thing is most fans don't pay any attention to that. They are only interested in wins and losses.

This was to be our biggest week to date. Our opponent, Big Walnut, was always one of the better teams that we played. This year would be no exception. They were coming into the game 5-1 and were a solid team. Although I had not voiced it to our guys, I didn't think that any of our victories this year had been over a good team. All three victories were over mediocre teams. We would be tested this week, and a victory would provide instant credibility for us. If we lost, it would signal people that we were improved, but not quite ready to play with "the big boys". Big Walnut was one of those boys.

Big Walnut was located in Sunbury, about fifty miles northeast of London. For decades what had been a small country town was rapidly growing as Columbus exploded northward. Plans were under way for the construction of a new high school to replace the one that they had recently been outgrown. The name Big Walnut is derived from a creek that meanders through town.

One aspect of our football team that had been a disappointment to us was our passing game. Although we had some very capable receivers and an excellent quarterback, we had not been able to develop a passing threat. Our four wins were a result of our ability to run the football. As a result, we had not been forced to throw the ball in critical situations. For weeks we had shared with the team that in order for us to win the rest of the games, we would have to develop a stronger passing game. After watching films of Big Walnut, I knew that if we were to win, this had to be the week that we broke loose.

With the Jonathan Alder game fresh in our mind, we formulated a positive approach to Big Walnut. We began on Monday to concentrate heavily on our passing game. We devoted almost the entire practice to passing. I took our quarterback aside and told him that this was the week that we had been waiting for and that I knew he was going to have the best game of his life. The week before, I had used my tongue to tear down our team. This week, I was going to use it to build it up. My attitude was not one of hope, but rather one of expectancy. I spoke confidence into them. I did the same thing with our receivers. I told them that they would be the difference in the game and that there was no way that Big Walnut would be able to cover them. Through positive expectations, we were going to make great things happen.

I knew that the key to our team was our quarterback, Joe Branson. He was the one person who would be able to elevate us to another level. Joey had all of the tools and was one of the hardest working kids I had ever coached. In the first half of the season, he had put too much pressure on himself by trying to do it all alone. I knew that he was ready to have a great game.

Up to that point, I don't believe that our football team had taken itself seriously. We knew that we were better than we were last year, but we were not convinced that we were good. It is so difficult, from a coaching standpoint, to try to control the attitude of your football team. Even though we worked hard on attitude, we couldn't filter what the athletes were hearing at home. No matter how much we built them up and encouraged them at practice, if they were being filled with negative expectations at school and at home, it would be difficult for us to overcome. The coaches knew we could beat Big Walnut, but what were the players hearing from their family and friends?

Friday, at school, I sensed a feeling among our team that I had not seen before. The kids were very focused on the game, and their classmates were genuinely supportive. There was an air of confidence around our kids that was exciting to see. We didn't hope to win; we expected to. I knew that we were in for a great night.

It was homecoming at Big Walnut, and they really do it up big. There was a festival-type attitude at the school as we arrived. Big Walnut students were dressed as Disney characters, and we were told that the game ball was to be brought in by a parachutist prior to kickoff. Based on recent history, we were clearly the underdog. We had come to play a football game, and we could tell that the Big Walnut team was caught up in all of the pageantry. An upset was in the making.

As we took the field to warm up for the game, we noticed a helicopter flying overhead in the clear, cloud speckled, autumn sky. It was a Central Ohio television station flying in to cover our football game.

"Hey! All of Central Ohio will see us kick their butts," Mike Fishman gruffly declared.

As we jogged onto the field, in my spirit, I could see the confidence and intensity level of our kids rise. I was hit with a sudden rush of pride.

"Everyone will see your team," Satan whispered in my ear. "You'll be a big deal." My spirit flashed a warning.

It became obvious to me that Satan had changed strategies. He knew that there was nothing that he could do to head off our victory, so he now chose another entryway into my life. He was trying to get me all puffed up in pride and self-glorification so that I would take full credit for the victory. Praise God, I was not ignorant to his devices!

As I walked among the rows of players during warm-up, I was thanking and praising Jesus for the victory that He had given us. I praised Him for the great coaches and players that He had given me, and for the miracles He had done and was continuing to do in my life. I asked Jesus to remove all prideful feelings from me and promised that, at the conclusion of the game, I would see that He received the credit.

As I stood at midfield, seemingly oblivious to the players and coaches involved in their pre-game drills, I was overcome with a feeling of release. I can't describe the cleansing that I felt. Christ had immediately taken all of those feelings away from me, and I knew that I had conquered the attack of pride upon me that night. The Lord was the one responsible for all of this, and I couldn't wait for the game to end so that I could share the story.

Our football team played exactly as I had known they would. Our quarterback had the best game of his career, and our wide receivers were devastating to the other team. Big Walnut was not prepared for our passing game. We jumped out to a 21-6 halftime lead and cruised to a 24-6 victory.

I was beside myself after the game. I circled among the players and coaches, exchanging bear hugs and slapping rear ends. So many things were running through my head. God's work in my life the past year was almost beyond belief. Psalm 37:23 says "The steps of a good man are ordered by the LORD: and he delighteth in his way. Though he fall, he shall not be utterly cast down: for the LORD upholdeth him with his hand."

I knew without a doubt that God was directing this football team and my life. Others may not understand why so many good things were happening to us, but I could feel God's hand.

I am reminded of the story of the ten lepers in Luke 17. Christ came upon these ten, and, in His mercy, He healed them of their infirmity. Of the ten lepers that were healed, only one even took the time to return and thank Christ for what He had done. The others went on about their business.

I did not want to be like that. I could list hundreds of things that Christ had done for me in the past year. Each one of them was a blessing. Was I going to be so ungrateful that I would not even take the time to thank Him? If I was to receive a present from someone, I would certainly take the time to let them know that I was appreciative. If others asked me where I had gotten the gift, I would explain who had given it to me. Should I be any less thankful of the gift that God had given me? I wanted everyone to know what I had and where I got it.

I make it a point every day to thank God for the many blessings that he has freely given me. If He were to stop giving me gifts today, I would be eternally grateful because He has given me far more than I deserve. Because I take the time to thank Him, I know that He will continue to give. I don't just thank Him for the gift today and then wait around to see what He will give me next. I am thankful and content in my spirit. God sees my heart.

As the football team gathered around me after the game, I looked up into the clear, sparkling night sky. I made sure that they heard me give the praise and glory to Jesus Christ. It wasn't that I expected them to agree with me, or to feel the same way that I felt. I wanted to make sure that God knew how I felt and that I was not ashamed to share it with others.

When I spoke with the newspaper reporters after the game, I made sure that I spoke boldly for Christ. They wanted to know what we had done to change our football team. They asked what kind of strategy had we used and all the basic questions that those in the world would want to know. I tried to explain that it was nothing that I had done, but I don't believe they understood.

When I opened up The Madison Press on Monday, I was pleased to read the article on our game. It appeared that the reporter had gotten the message. To quote from the article,

"The coaching staff did a tremendous job," Daubenmire said. "I don't take any credit for it. I thank Jesus Christ for giving me good coaches and a great group of kids to work with."

We were 5-2 and in sole possession of second place. We controlled our destiny. If we won our last three games, we would win the championship. As we boarded the two yellow school buses for the exciting trip home, somehow I knew that the challenges ahead would not be easy

WINNERS AT LAST

Ephesians 3:20 "Now unto him that is able to do exceeding abundantly above all that we ask or think, according to the power that worketh in us,"

There was an unbelievable change in the attitude of our football team following the victory over Big Walnut. It was as though we had finally come of age. I know that our players had wanted to win the game, but I am not sure if we really believed that we could. After soundly beating what we knew was a good team, our kids were brimming with confidence. It wasn't the cocky "I'm somebody" type of confidence, but rather a belief in themselves and their teammates.

A big problem that we had faced since I was at London finally began to change. I have mentioned earlier that our athletes really did not feel special. Because success had been hard to come by, many of our athletes were ashamed of the fact that they were athletes. They played sports because they enjoyed them, but they did not feel that they had the respect of their classmates. We had talked to them about the importance of acting differently from the non-athletic students. It takes a lot of courage for a young person to stand up for something that he or she knows is right. Peer pressure is a strong force, and many of our kids were not able to overcome it. Their confidence level and self image was just not high enough.

Alcohol use is a big problem in our schools. The only schools who don't believe they have problems with it are the ones who deny its existence. At London, we had chosen to no longer do that. We introduced into all of the athletic teams a program called Clique 1. The purpose of this program was to rid our teams of alcohol and drug use. This would not be easy, but we were committed to attacking this thing head-on.

Briefly, Clique 1 is a network of parents, coaches and players working together to be drug and alcohol free. Our society sends so many mixed messages to our young people that it is no surprise that they are confused. With all of the beer commercials on T.V., and all of the professional athletes promoting its use, our kids have gotten the idea that to be an athlete requires the use of alcohol. There was a day when athletics was the main reason kids did not drink. Today it has become the major reason why young people do drink. The purpose of the Clique 1 program was to change attitudes of parents, coaches, and players about the use of alcohol. We needed to let the kids know that we expected them not to drink and use drugs. If they chose to be an athlete, then they would have to say no to drugs. Only by working together can parents, coaches, and athletes bring about these changes.

Nothing will ever change unless we first change attitudes. All of the programs in the world are useless if you cannot change the heart of a man. Our Clique 1 program had been in effect all year, and I believed that our athletes had been drug and alcohol free during the season. They followed the rules because they had committed to each other, not because they felt they were special. After the Big Walnut game, I felt for the first time that our football players felt special, and the Clique 1 program was working to show them that they didn't need alcohol or drugs as they thought they had during our summer camping trip.

The attitude in our whole school had changed. I heard a long time ago that you could tell what kind of football season a school was having just by walking in the door. That was true at our school. Where the attitude the year before had been somber and defeatist, the halls that year were alive and full of spirit. It was exciting to see our student body begin to support our football team. Even the students who were usually not interested in anything, suddenly began to talk about the football team. It made our athletes proud, and they were raising the standards in our entire school.

I had tried to tell anyone who would listen that our leadership problem was not the kids' faults. It was a fault of the system. Each year the coaches would sit around and moan and groan about the lack of senior leadership. For some reason, we thought that all of a sudden when an athlete became a senior, he was supposed to be a leader. It just does not work that way. Our seniors had learned how to be leaders by watching the class ahead of them. Because we had not been successful for so long, it had been a long time since we had great leadership. It is the old catch-22 problem. We would never win until our leadership got better; and our leadership would not get better until we won. Our leadership had not been great for several years, but that was not the fault of the athletes. It is our job to give them the proper direction.

Our mixed messages had been very confusing to them. Just think about our attitudes a minute. We tell our kids not to drink, but if they do, don't drive. A kid reads that as our saying it is okay to drink. We tell kids not to smoke because it is bad for them and then we continue to do it. We ask our kids to be reliable and make a commitment and then they stand by and watch fifty percent of our marriages end in divorce. This do- as-I-say-not-as-I-do attitude is phony and kids see right through it. The leadership problem is not with kids, it is with adults.

This had been my contention back in June when we had the drinking episode at our camp-out. I couldn't believe that they had done it, but I knew it wasn't their fault. Somehow we had to be able to get across to these kids that there was a right and wrong, and that it was our responsibility to live our lives according to those principles. It was gratifying to me to see that these young men were now becoming the leaders that we had hoped they would be. Because of the leadership of this group, I am convinced that the attitude at London High School had changed. I give all of the credit to Christ. He was able to take that horrible night in June and make something good out of it.

Our opponent this week was Bexley High School. Bexley was not having a great year, but they were very well coached and always played hard. One of my worst memories of coaching was the Bexley game the year before. It had been the last game of the season my first year at London. They had a great running back who had eaten us alive. Our team had fallen apart the last half of the season, and we reached rock bottom against Bexley that night. The final score was 48-16, but that was not the most disturbing part. Our kids played out of control. We played dirty and were clearly frustrated. At the end of the game, we had parents swearing at coaches, players swearing at each other, and parents swearing at parents. It was a real nightmare. Satan had drug me through the mud that night and he had me at an all-time low. I was sad to admit that the program was no further along than when I had first taken the job. In fact, I think we had regressed. What a difference a year made!

Bexley is a town very similar to Grandview Heights located on the near east side of downtown Columbus. It is one of the more affluent neighborhoods in all of Columbus. Most of the families are well educated, and Bexley is the home of Capital University. The town is characterized by older homes situated on clean, tree-lined streets. We always sensed that Bexley played us with their collective nose in the air, as if it were beneath them to even be on the same field with us. Our guys hated that attitude.

Our week of preparation for the game had gone well. The confidence that we had gained from the previous week really began to manifest itself. It was exciting to see our players working hard in practice. They were not content with what they had done, but were hungry for more. We had three very tough games ahead of us, but we had improved greatly in the past month and I saw nothing to indicate that we were going to rest on our laurels. That previous Sunday at church, God had put my heart at rest.

As I previously mentioned, World Harvest Church is an amazing place to be. It is impossible to attend service there and not be touched in some way by the Holy Spirit. One never seems to know what to expect because Pastor Rod is led by the Holy Spirit. I always leave there changed.

The Sunday after the Big Walnut game was no exception. We have a thirty piece orchestra and a choir that leads our Praise and Worship at church. The music is used as an entryway into the presence of God. Psalm 100:4 says "Enter His gates with thanksgiving, and into His courts with praise." I stood there in church with my thoughts on the goodness of the Lord and offered up thanks along with 3000 other souls. The Holy Spirit spoke to Pastor Parsley to encourage us to ask the Lord for the desires of our hearts, and that the Spirit was there to draw us closer to the Lord. Without having preplanned my prayer, I asked the Lord to grant our football team three more wins so that we could be Central Buckeye League Champions. I asked that he would exalt us so that we could in turn exalt Him. He answered my prayer. I didn't hear a voice, but I knew that my prayer had been answered. I can't explain it.

I was very proud of our football team that Friday night. We went about our job in a very business-like fashion. Our offense the past few weeks had been hitting on all cylinders and we continued to execute against Bexley. Our running game was as consistent as it had been all season, and our passing game continued to blossom. Bexley had geared their defense to stop our running game, and we were able to throw the ball for almost two hundred yards. Although our defense had two breakdowns that enabled Bexley's quarterback to break loose for two long runs, Coach Emmets had them playing another solid game. We walked off of the field as winners with a 35-19 victory. The scene was set for our championship football game against Dublin the next Friday night.

It was something that many of the kids had only dreamed about, and now it was going to be a reality.

After our homecoming victory over Grandview, the London band had led the team back to the locker room. It was about a half mile walk, but we had walked as the band played the fight song. Again that night, the police shut down High Street, stopping all traffic on the main drag through London as we marched through town together. It was exciting to see so much pride as the town came to life. Red Raider spirit was alive and well. After a decade of remission, our football team had resurrected the London spirit.

We were 6-2 and assured of a winning record. For the first time in my ten year career as a head coach, I had won more than I had lost. Mark Collier and I walked together as we left the field.

"Mark, this is the first time I've ever won six games," I said over the noise of the band.

"I know," he answered. "I was going to mention it earlier in the week but I didn't want to bring it up. I knew that you were aware of it."

I reached out and wrapped my short, stocky arm around his broad shoulders.

"I'm glad you're here, Mark. I just knew it could be like this. I knew we would have a great team," I continued.

"Daub, this is just how you said it would be, way back in May. This is what you said. It's been great."

"Take my word for it, Mark," I said. "We're not done yet."

As I looked down High Street I saw the street lined with cheering fans, waving red and white banners. People of all ages joined in our march through the heart of town. At each intersection cars sat and honked their horns and people yelled encouragement. I felt a great sense of satisfaction. This was why I had become a coach. Not for the glory, but rather, for the impact that I could have on others. We were involved in something bigger than a football season. We were changing this town. It had happened so fast that no man could take credit. I Corinthians 2:9 states But as it is written, Eye hath not seen, nor ear heard, neither have entered into the heart of man, the things which God hath prepared for them that love him."

I was about to embark on the most incredible week of my life.

Making the Devil's Hit List

*Ephesians 6:13 Wherefore take unto you the whole armour of
God, that ye may be able to withstand in the evil day, and
having done all, to stand."*

What are you supposed to do when a goal that you had
worked so hard to attain was finally within your grasp? We
found ourselves on the threshold of our first ever Central Buckeye
League championship. Months earlier, this had started as a dream
conceived within the heart of a few men, and now the moment was
upon us. Our task was clear, but it would not be easy. If our football team was able to defeat the Dublin Shamrocks on Friday
night, we would be assured of no worse than a tie for the league
championship.

Dublin was the largest school in our league. They had won
the last two Central Buckeye League championships and were
determined to make it three in a row in this, the last year ever for

the C.B.L. At the end of the season, the league was disbanding as several schools had sought other league affiliations. Because of the growth of these schools within the league, the C.B.L. had become out of balance. Whoever won the league this year would be defending champions forever.

Dublin is one of the fastest growing suburbs in all of central Ohio. The city of Dublin was once a small rural town much like London. In the previous ten years, the city of Columbus had exploded to the north. Most of the residents are employed in high paying white-collar jobs. Dublin has now become the epitome of yuppieville. There are more BMW cars in Dublin than there are people in London.

The town had grown so quickly that the size of the high school had more than quadrupled in size. Because they were so much larger than any other school in the league, they had won the league championship the past three years. This would be the last year in the league as they were moving to a league that had much larger schools. Future Ohio State Buckeye recruiting coordinator Bill Conley was their very able coach.

Our kids especially did not like Dublin because of the arrogance that their players exuded. The previous year, Dublin had come to play us at vonKanel Field with over one hundred players. They had so many players that we could not even fit them all into our locker room. Our forty players were intimidated as the seas of green and white clad players flowed onto the field. After they beat us, the players began to chant at our players as they left the field.

"That's all right, that's o.k. You're going to work for us someday."

I had received an ominous sign at church the following Sunday. My mother had shared with some people at World Harvest the article from The Madison Press where credit had been given to Jesus Christ for the victory. Although they were all rejoicing because it had appeared in print, one of the women gave my mother a word of warning.

"Tell your son that he needs to brace for an onslaught of the enemy," she said. "Satan is really angry about the work that he is doing in London, and he should know that he has just moved up on the devil's hit list."

Not exactly the type of news that you would want to hear, wouldn't you agree? There we were, involved in the biggest week of our season, and God was sending word to me that there was trouble on the horizon. I was not scared because I knew that nothing could separate me from the love of God. God promises us in I Corinthians 10:13 that He will not allow us to be tempted beyond what we will be able to endure. I knew that He had given me victory over Satan and all of his devices and that I would have to prepare myself for the battle. Without the battle, there is no victory.

Monday at school I could already see Satan beginning to do his work. The attitude surrounding our kids at school was flippant and disrespectful. Even though their classmates were excited and interested in the upcoming game, our athletes did not seem to be concentrating on the task at hand. My spirit was alert and attuned to what was going on around us. I could sense the presence of a new spirit, but I could not put my finger on just what it was. That afternoon at practice, it surfaced.

After about a month of great practices, our football team had its worst practice of the year that afternoon. Our team unity seemed to have dissipated, and the kids were argumentative and uncooperative. I didn't overreact, but, at the conclusion of practice, I asked the seniors to stay for a meeting.

As the coaches gathered the seniors around us, I prayed for the right words to say. The fields around the school were beginning to take on the look of winter as the farmers had been working for the past week to harvest the corn that encircled the school. The boys were especially quiet as they dropped to one knee in a semicircle around us. Many leaned forward with their eyes down and rested their hand upon their red helmet.

"Ok, guys," I said. "What the heck is going on? Here it is, the biggest week of your life, and you guys are acting like a bunch of babies. Somebody tell me what's going on."

I searched their faces for some clue. I tried to catch their eye, hoping that one of them would open up. I silently prayed for the Holy Spirit.

"Are you nervous?" I asked searching for a clue.

"Yes I am, Coach," one of them finally volunteered.

"About what? Losing? Playing poorly? What?" I asked.

"I'm just tired of the crap," he continued, "That is all everybody is talking about, the game Friday night. How they all hope we win and how great it will be if we can be

C.B.L. champions. I'm tired of hearing about it."

"Yeah," another one joined in. "It used to be fun, all the attention and everything, but now there seems like there is so much pressure on us that I just wish the game would hurry up and get here."

"Are you afraid we'll get beat?" I asked.

"No, I'm not afraid of that. I just don't know how long I can listen to all of it. I just want to be an ordinary student again."

We talked for about ten minutes about how we felt. It was a situation that our athletes were not used to. It was good that we were able to share those feelings with each other because we found out that many of us felt the same way. The players all agreed that they could make it three more days, and that we should not allow the wants and desires of others to interfere with the job that we had to do. We had earned the right to be in this game, and we needed to play this game for ourselves, not for our school. We left the field in a playful mood, but that didn't last very long.

As a group of the players were walking off the field together, they began to tease each other and take part in a little horseplay. It seemed harmless enough. Before we knew it, Kenny and Bubba were rolling around on the ground, and it was obvious that this was not in jest. As their teammates separated the two, they continued screaming at each other. All the way to the locker room, they were struggling to get back at each other. It was so bad that I didn't feel that I could let the two of them go into the locker room at the same time. They both hopped into their cars and sped out of the parking lot, one giving chase to the other.

No one could understand what had just happened. It was just an example of the tenseness that was gripping our team. Throughout the whole thing I had remained calm. I knew just who it was that we were fighting, and I was not going to lose my focus this week. I understood that this was a spiritual attack, and I knew how to fight it. I was careful not to overreact to this episode. Satan cannot read a person's mind. He could only react to what I said or did, and I was not going to give him an indication that he was affecting our team. I turned it over to God and assured Him that I knew that He was directing our team.

That was only one of the prongs of the spiritual attack. Earlier that day, I had received a call from my wife that my son was sick with the flu, and that I would have to go to school and get him. I wasn't worried about his illness, but someone had to be home with him. Since my wife worked also, I decided to go home even though I didn't like to miss work. This was especially true during the football season because I liked to be there to keep an eye on the players.

The next day everything seemed to be okay. The two players were friends again, and the incident seemed to be forgotten. Unfortunately, the sickness that Zack had, now dug its claws into me. I tried to go to school, but was only able to make it half a day. I had a severe case of the flu. My head ached, I was nauseated, and I had a bad case of the flu. I was quite a sight. Here I was trying to prepare for the biggest game of my life, and I couldn't even keep my eyes open. Tuesday and Wednesday I was able to make it into school in the mornings, only to crawl home at noon to try and sleep for a couple of hours. I would get up in time to make it back to practice, but I couldn't do much coaching. I spent most of my energy trying not to throw up or go sit on the commode. Thank God I had great assistant coaches. Sickness at any time is hard to handle, but with the actions of our football players that week, it was almost too much to overcome.

I knew who the enemy was. I cursed him and everything that he stood for. I did not waste my time in self-pity and fear. I knew that God was going to bring me through this week, and there would be victory on the other side. I reminded myself of what I had learned in church. When you are going through something, just stand firm, because you are going through. You will eventually make it to the other side. I couldn't wait to see what God had planned for me once I made it through, because the spiritual attack was so strong, I knew that something great had to be waiting on the other side.

Up until that week, the unity on our football team had been remarkable. Anytime you get forty players together, you are bound to have personality clashes, but we had kept them to a minimum that year. That week, however, the enemy of our soul was working overtime to disrupt us.

Although our concentration appeared to be better on Tuesday, our guys were still super-sensitive. Whenever a player was criticized it seemed to be taken personally. It was difficult to do any coaching because the kids were so uptight that anytime we corrected them, they responded with anger and self-pity. My natural reaction was to grab them and shake them. I chose to do just the opposite.

Because of my physical condition, I was wearing sunglasses during practice. This cut down on the glare of the sun and made practice more bearable. Our team could not see my eyes as they searched me for a reaction to their sudden outbursts. I was unshakable in my faith. I knew that by resisting the enemy, he would have to flee. The more the kids misbehaved, the more I lifted up my spirit in prayer.

Toward the end of practice, our twin tackles, Aundrey and Kenny, got into a shouting match on the way back to the huddle. I didn't know what had caused the disagreement, but I was sure that it was something minor. Before we knew it, they were screaming and hollering, digging up every negative thing about each other that they could think of. Within seconds, they were entangled on the ground trying to separate the other's head from his shoulders. Their teammates dived into the middle and broke it up and dragged them screaming back toward the huddle.

I never said a word about what had happened. I merely substituted two players and continued on with practice. Aundrey walked to one side of the field and put on his best Ninja face, and Kenny went the other way to find a teammate to commiserate with. The players on the team had to wonder what was going on. I am usually very aggressive in attacking problems, especially the type that we were facing now. Instead, I acted as if nothing had happened and continued on with practice.

On Wednesday, Curtis, our big receiver, went bonkers. We were finishing up practice by working on our passing game, and he did not run the correct pattern. In a great deal of our passing game, we gave the receiver an option to run one of two patterns, depending on the defensive alignment that he saw. On this particular play, the rules were changed and he had to run the pass cut, a slant, which had been called in the huddle. Curtis saw where the defender was lined up and changed the pattern on his own. The quarterback threw the ball where the receiver should have been, and it was intercepted. I calmly approached him and tried to instruct him.

"Curtis, whenever we call a slant you cannot check into something else. No matter where the defender lines up, you are going to have to work toward the inside of him. As big as you are, it will be impossible for him to stop you without interfering."

I don't believe he heard a word that I said. As he approached me he had a wide- eyed look on his face. The whites of his eyes seemed as large as saucers, accentuated against his deep black skin. He began to yell at me.

"Just because I'm not a senior, it's my fault. All of these other guys can screw up, and nobody ever says anything to them. But let me do something wrong, and you jump all over me," he screamed. Anger flashed in his eyes, and spit spewed out of his mouth.

"I'm not jumping on you, Curtis. I just don't want you to make that mistake in the game," I returned matter-of-factly.

He just exploded at me. He began to scream at me about how I was picking on him. He ranted and raved and stomped around, screaming things that made no sense to anybody there. He finished his tirade, looked directly in my face, and said something that a player should never say to an adult. Anger swelled in my chest as he challenged me in front of all of his teammates. I could feel 80 eyes bore into my soul. I prayed softly for peace, and took in a deep breath.

"Get somebody in there for him," I said calmly. "Now let's huddle up and do it right."

I learned a few years ago that the only person who can control my attitude is me. I determine how I will react, what I will say, and what will be done. It would be wrong for me to relinquish that power to someone else. Whenever we react to the things that are going on around us, we have given control of our attitude to that person or thing. God was in control of this situation. When a volatile situation occurred, I acknowledged the strength of God within me and remained in control of my natural desires. I would not give Satan control of this team.

Did our team view me as weak? I don't think so. They knew me well enough to know what I would and would not put up with. They knew this was a special set of circumstances, and I knew that my strength in the middle of this chaos was what was needed.

We received a break with our schedule at school. We were not having school on Thursday or Friday of that week. London High School was having parent-teacher conferences on Tuesday and Wednesday nights. This required the teachers to stay at school until 9:00 p.m. In return, there would be no school on Thursday to make up for the extra time put in. Friday was a day off in all of Central Ohio due to COTA day, which was a day used for teacher in-service and instruction. Those two days off school were a blessing in more ways than one.

My physical strength was really down. The flu had sapped me of all of my energy. I had not been able to eat all week, and the stomach problems would not go away. During parent-teacher conferences, I had to excuse myself several times to go to the rest-room. I felt awful. I needed to get some rest so that I could shake this thing off. The chance to sleep-in on Thursday and Friday mornings was something that could not have come at a better time.

The day off of school really helped our football team, too. They were relieved to not have to go to school and listen to their classmates chatter about Friday night's game. It was a different team that came to practice Thursday afternoon. The day off had given them a much needed mental break, and much of the tension had been relieved. We kept practice short and upbeat, and, for the first time all week, I noticed some of the boys laughing and enjoying themselves.

It had become our custom on Thursday nights to eat a team meal that had been prepared by the parents. As I mentioned earlier, a lot of our players did not socialize together, and these meals gave us the opportunity to be together in a relaxing atmosphere. The meals did wonders for our team unity.

Every week we invited someone to speak to our team after the meal. We had focused on former players and coaches in the community who could help our players become more aware of the great tradition in London. This week, because of my own illness, I had not made firm plans with our speaker, and he had other commitments. I found out on Wednesday evening that he would not be able to attend. As I lay in bed reading the Bible before I went to sleep, God gave me the message that I would deliver to the team the next evening.

After a turbulent week filled with distractions and sickness, we needed a fresh touch. The Holy Spirit gave me a message that was would be forever stamped in the hearts of those young men. We would need all the help we could get.

ROCKS

John 8:7 "So when they continued asking him, he lifted up himself, and said unto them, He that is without sin among you, let him first cast a stone at her."

B oy was I glad to see that week come to an end. The spiritual attack upon me had been relentless, and it still would not let go. The flu that I picked up on Monday was still hanging on. Because my energy level was so low, I had not spent enough time in prayer during the week. If I had, I believe that I would have been able to head off some of the attack before it ever got started. I knew that prayer was the answer to all of my problems, but the turmoil had drained me so badly in a physical sense that it took away from my ability to pray. All I wanted to do was sleep. I couldn't do the spiritual warfare necessary to bring the battle to an end. James 5:15 declares "And the prayer of faith shall save the sick,"

My attitudes regarding healing have changed. I was not raised in a home or a church where divine healing was practiced. For some reason, many Christians do not believe that it is God's plan for us to be healthy. Many times I have asked people if they believed that God could heal them only to hear them respond, "I believe He could if He wanted to."

It is obvious that we do not understand the will of God. God can and will do all things. The Bible lists at least twenty specific physical healings that Jesus performed. In fact, it is almost commonplace in the four gospels. Physical healing was one of the major focuses of Christ's ministry, yet it is the one miracle that is least believed in the world today. The Bible states that God is no respecter of persons. What He has done for one person, He will do for another. If He healed the centurion's servant, then He will heal me, too. That is His promise.

I used to watch and laugh at the Faith Healers that I would see on T.V. My youngest brother became great at imitating Ernest Angley as he laid hands on people and cast out demons. We used to laugh at him and the fools who sent him money. Of course, we were Christians, but this healing stuff was stupid and just a way for some preachers to get rich. An incident with my sister changed my view on healing.

In 1985, my only sister, Jane, was diagnosed with cancer of the uterus. She had the diagnosis confirmed by several doctors and was scheduled for a hysterectomy. One evening a friend of hers invited her to World Harvest Church where she experienced the true presence of God for the first time. After her first visit, she didn't know what she thought of this church, but she definitely knew there was something different about it. When she returned a second time, she was called out by Pastor Parsley, and the congregation prayed for her. She was, at that moment, instantaneously healed of her cancer. She went ahead and had her surgery, explaining to the doctor that she had been healed. After the surgery, the doctor told her that they had found no trace of the disease in her body!

My sister is the oldest of my parents' five children. Like all of us, she was raised a Catholic and faithfully attended Mass as a young girl. When she married her first husband, she became a Lutheran so that she and her husband would be equally yoked. The marriage lasted eleven years until she could no longer deal with his steady drinking. After five years of being on her own, she remarried a fine moral man named Karl. It was shortly after this that the cancer attacked her body, and her own spiritual conversion took place.

At this time, I was not saved, and to say the least, this got my attention. I thought that she had lost her mind. Healed by God? She must be some kind of kook. I had no proof of her physical healing, but I could tell that there was something different about her. She began to attend church on Sunday nights and Wednesday nights, and her conversation was laced with references to Jesus. No one could deny the change in her. After running out of excuses, I finally accepted an invitation to go to church with her. Needless to say, it was not long before I, too, had become a believer.

Because of the experience my sister had, I knew the flu that I had was not from God. It was not something that He had given me to teach me a lesson, or something that He had given me to make me stronger. It was stupid to think that God would cause me to become ill, and, at the same time, expect me to serve Him in my job here in London. This sickness was an attack upon my body. I had the power through Jesus Christ to cast that sickness out of my body. I knew that, and I believed it. If God could take cancer out of my sister, how tough could a flu virus be for Him? I had become so preoccupied with our football team and the problems associated with it that I had not taken authority over the sickness. I had permitted it to remain in my body. I had not used the power that Christ had given to me.

Instead, I had repeated some silly prayer about being healed, but I had not committed my heart to it. I did not believe the prayer that I was saying. It became merely a vain repetition and did me absolutely no good. The key to receiving, is believing. Mark 9:23 tells us "If thou canst believe, all things are possible to him that believeth." I can pray all day long, but if I do not believe what I am praying, then my prayers are powerless.

After practice Thursday, my son Zack and I went to the freshman game. There is a stream that runs behind the grandstand at our stadium, and along the banks of that creek are a lot of flat rocks. I took a bucket and asked Zack to fill it up with rocks for me. He enjoyed playing down by the river, so he was happy to do it. It wasn't long before he brought the bucket up and gave it to me.

We were playing Dublin, and their nickname was the Shamrocks. When their new coach had arrived on the scene, he shortened the name to 'Rocks. It had become a trademark for them signifying their toughness. Our players knew that the bucket full of rocks had something to do with Dublin. They kept asking me what they were for, but I told them that they would just have to wait and see. Little did they know it had nothing to do with the Dublin Shamrocks.

That night following the team meal I gathered the team together in the school's auditorium for a meeting. I stationed one of our captains at the entrance of the room and had him hand out a rock to everyone as they entered. The kids were in a jovial mood as they gathered in the room, and they tossed the rocks up and down in the air and made jokes about bashing each other with them. As I made my way to the front of the room, I asked the Holy Spirit to anoint the message He had given me.

Our auditorium was connected to the lunch room. It was a nice facility that we used many times during the year because it made it better for the athletes to be a captive audience. It has about three hundred fold-down theatre seats. All of the players settled into the middle section, and the seniors always sat in the front row. Since we had begun these meetings, they wanted to be close. Acting like sponges, they soaked up the wisdom that was weekly shared with them. Using the brown curtains upon the stage as a backdrop, I moved before the team.

"Listen up, men. I know that we are all ready to play this football game tomorrow, and I know what a difficult week this has been for all of us. I know that you are used to having guest speakers, but I have reserved this night for me.

"You guys know how I am. Whenever I am looking for inspiration and guidance, I turn to the Bible." I reached in my pocket and pulled out a pocket New Testament.

"I'd like to share with you a story from the Gospel of John. Back in the days of Christ they believed in immediate punishment of crimes. If you were found guilty of breaking the law, then punishment would occur that day. One of the means of enforcing the death penalty was to stone someone to death. They would corner the guilty person and continue to throw stones at him until he was dead. Let me read John 8 verses 1-11:

"Jesus went unto the mount of Olives. And early in the morning he came again into the temple, and all the people came unto him; and he sat down, and taught them. And the scribes and Pharisees brought unto him a woman taken in adultery; and when they had set her in the midst, They say unto him, Master, this woman was taken in adultery, in the very act. Now Moses in the law commanded us, that such should be stoned: but what sayest thou? This they said, tempting him, that they might have to accuse him. But Jesus stooped down, and with his finger wrote on the ground, as though he heard them not. So when they continued asking him, he lifted up himself, and said unto them, He that is without sin among you, let him first cast a stone at her. And again he stooped down, and wrote on the ground. And they which heard it, being convicted by their own conscience, went out one by one, beginning at the eldest, even unto the last: and Jesus was left alone, and the woman standing in the midst. When Jesus had lifted up himself, and saw none but the woman, he said unto her, Woman, where are those thine accusers? hath no man condemned thee? She said, No man, Lord. And Jesus said unto her, Neither do I condemn thee: go, and sin no more."

The mood in the room had suddenly turned somber. The kids assumed that they knew why I had given them the rocks. Slowly, the realization was coming to them that these rocks were for an entirely different purpose.

"The easiest thing in the world for us to do is to criticize and blame and point our fingers at others," I continued. "We have gotten to where we are because we have hung together. None of us are perfect or have played perfectly this year. We have refused to get down on one another, knowing that mentally beating up our buddy doesn't take any courage. We have made it where we are together, as a family.

"Stand up, Joey."

Our quarterback rose slowly to his feet and stood before his teammates. He shuffled his feet nervously, and his eyes darted from me to the floor and back. I surveyed the group before me and bore in.

"Tomorrow night in the game, Joe may throw an interception or have a fumble at a crucial time. He may do something really stupid that may penalize us all. He's human; he's nervous. It is the biggest game of his life. How will you respond if he screws up?"

I zeroed in on Aundrey, and moved over in front of him until only a foot separated our faces.

"How about you Aundrey, have you ever missed a block? Have you ever jumped off sides? Have you ever allowed your man to get loose and blast Joey from the backside?"

'Drey was one of our more volatile members, and here I was challenging him before his teammates. His ninja face was even more puckered than usual. I immediately thought back to that morning when he had been forced to run 6 miles in the rain, and how deep his commitment to his teammates had become.

"Yes, I have," he responded meekly as his eyes searched the floor. Beads of sweat seeped out of his chocolate forehead.

"That's right! You have and you may miss one tomorrow night," I continued. "Unless you have played the perfect game, you keep your mouth shut. Do you understand that, Drey? You do your job; trust Joe to do his."

"Yes, sir, I understand," was his firm, humble reply.

I turned back to Joe.

"Do you think he will screw up on purpose, Joe? Do you think he would purposely let you down? Since that day he ran in the rain, he has given us everything he has. Do you think he would purposely let you down now?"

Joe's face had drained to the same color as his blonde, wavy hair, and he looked piercingly at Aundrey.

"I know you'll do your best, Drey, and so will I." Tears filled their eyes as this dedicated, blond-headed leader, walked over and bear-hugged his huge, man-boy, buddy.

"Stand up Doug." I barked out.

The anointing was so thick in that room that I could feel it. Every eye was focused on me. Players were no longer slumped in their seats, but rather, sitting upright as if straining to hear the next word.

"Are you going to play hard out there tomorrow, Doug?" I asked. Doug was our starting safety.

"Yes, Sir," he responded nervously as he chewed on his lip.

"If a receiver beats you deep tomorrow night, is it going to be because you wanted him to? After all that you have put into this season, are you going to go out there tomorrow night and screw up on purpose?" I asked, knowing the question was ridiculous.

"I'm going to give it all I got, Coach," he answered as his brown eyes flashed determination. Some players' eyes darted to the floor, fearful that they might be the one challenged next.

My eyes moved back and forth through the group, pausing just long enough to let our souls connect. My eyes returned and focused on our inside linebacker, Mike Fishman.

"If Doug gets beat, Fish, what are you going to do? Are you going to start running your mouth at him? Are you going to tell him how lousy he is and how much he has let us all down? Don't you think he already knows that? Does he need you to tell him that? Does he?"

"No, He don't need to hear that," came his reply as he set his firm, square jaw. I could see his tenseness as the muscles in his face twitched. Beads of sweat were forming on his upper lip.

"No!" I screamed, forcing the veins to bulge out on my neck. "He doesn't need to hear that from you or anyone else on this team. You keep your mouth shut. Do you understand, Mike? Do you guys all understand?"

My eyes scoured the room for effect.

Slowly, I stretched out my hand toward Mike and extended him the large rock that I held.

"If you are going to throw stones at Doug, then let's not wait until tomorrow. Let's do it right now. Let's all blast Doug so bad that we break his spirit. What use will he be to us tomorrow? We can't afford to do it to him now or during the game. We need him. We need what Doug has to offer. We need what you all have to offer. If he screws up, Fish, could you keep the stone in your pocket and do something that will help pick his spirits up? Will you encourage him?"

Fish took his eyes off of me and focused on his buddy Doug. He extended his hand and squeezed Doug's.

"You can count on me, Fresh. We can do it if we hang together," he said as his voice cracked. "I ain't going to let you down."

Red eyes were blinking all across the auditorium.

"I'll do my job," Doug committed in front of his teammates. "Let's all just do our job."

"Sit down, Doug," I spoke softly.

Again, I looked into the eyes of this group of young men and tried to see into their souls. Each boy returned my gaze as if he were doing the same to me. Spirit to spirit, we locked in.

"Dublin is not our opponent tomorrow," I continued. "We play this football game against ourselves. Bad things are going to happen to both teams out there tomorrow night. The team that will win will be the one who sticks together. If you have never made a mistake, then you have a right to throw your rock as often and as hard as you can. But if you have screwed up before, then you have no business even reaching for your pocket."

What a feeling was in that room! The Holy Spirit had driven it home. I paused to let the impact settle in.

"I want you to take that rock home with you tonight and set it on your dresser or some other place where you can see it, and before you go to bed, stop and think about what you have heard tonight. Bring the rock to school with you tomorrow. Carry it around as a reminder of how we are going to play together. Tomorrow night, when we get back from the game at Dublin, we are going to build a monument out of the rocks that we didn't throw, as a lasting sign of what can be accomplished if we will only work together."

I stared deeply into the eyes of many of the young men. These young boys had come so far.

"We love you guys and the great effort that you have given us. Dream great dreams, stay together, and tomorrow all of your hard work will be rewarded."

There was electricity in that room as the players sat and let the magnitude of what they had just heard sink in. As they quietly left the school, rocks in hand, I knew that we were one, both in body and spirit.

"Coach." It was Norm Emmets. "I've never heard anything like that before. Something just happened here, Coach. I can't explain it, but I can feel it. Something happened."

"I know 'E'. You had to be dead not to feel it. Something great is going to happen."

The flu had refused to loosen its grip upon my body. Although my headache and fever were gone, there still was queasiness in my stomach that would not allow me to eat. As I lay down to sleep that night, I was hopeful that a good night's sleep would help me to awaken feeling better.

After about an hour of sleep, I was awakened by a violent rumbling in my stomach. I leaped from my bed, rushed to the bathroom and was attacked by a sever case of diarrhea. I couldn't believe that it was possible for anything to come out of my body because I hadn't eaten all week. For the next four hours I had to hurry to the restroom in ten-minute intervals. Never before had I experienced anything like it.

I could tell that sleep was going to be impossible. In between trips to the restroom, I began to read from scripture. I wasn't really reading any part of it in particular, but instead I was jumping around to different verses that I had underlined in my Bible. After about my tenth trip to the bathroom, I returned to bed and opened my Bible to Isaiah 53:5 "But he was wounded for our transgressions, he was bruised for our iniquities: the chastisement of our peace was upon him; and with his stripes we are healed." Immediately, I heard a voice within me say, "How long are you going to put up with this."

I jumped out of bed and began to thank and praise Jesus for the healing that he had given to me. I realized that I had not really focused in on believing what I had been asking. Those words seared into my spirit. I cursed Satan and commanded him that in the name of Jesus Christ he must flee from my body. I declared that my body was the temple of the Holy Spirit and that it was off limits to him. I repeated Isaiah 53:5 to him and told him that he was defeated in my life. Sickness and disease had no hold over me because of the power of Jesus Christ alive within me. As I prayed, I was hit with the urge to go to the restroom again. I continued to pray as I made my way there. This trip to the toilet was different. It was as if the Lord was flushing my system. I literally could feel all of that sickness leave my body. I returned to my bed, turned off the light, and fell soundly to sleep. It was 4:00 a.m. I awakened at 10:00a.m. the next morning feeling healthy and alert. I had weathered the storm.

CHAMPIONS

*I Corinthians 9:24 Know ye not that they which
run in a race run all, but one receiveth the prize?
So run, that ye may obtain."*

I arrived at the school early to get ready for the game. It was hard to believe that I felt as good as I did considering what my body had been through the past week. As I mentioned earlier, we did not have school on Friday, and that seemed to make the day drag on. I was anxious to go to battle.

It was a confident group of football players that arrived that evening. Many of the players arrived at the school carrying their rocks. I was especially pleased when one of the seniors came up to me and told me that he had slept with the rock under his pillow. I knew that the message from the night before had sunk in.

Dublin High School had the nicest football facility in all of central Ohio. It was hard to go play in that stadium without feeling intimidated. The playing surface was plush, the grandstands were huge, the locker rooms were massive, and to top it off, they had an electronic, computerized scoreboard! The very atmosphere sends a message that you are playing somebody better than you.

We arrived early so that our players would have the chance to become acclimated to the surroundings. I didn't want us to react like a group of country boys who were making their first trip to the city. By having extra time to walk around the field, our players had a chance to let the shock of this beautiful facility wear off. When we finally entered into the locker room for our pre-game preparation, I was confident that our kids were focused on the game. We were not intimidated.

At 6:05 we took the field for the pre-game warm-up, I was overcome with feelings of love and pride for these young men. They had overcome seemingly insurmountable odds to be poised for this championship attempt. The players took their places on the field for stretching, and I moved in the midst of them. I had never done before what I did then. One by one, I went down the line, looked each of them in the eye, called them by name and said, "I love you." Some of them said, "I love you, too, Coach" or "Thanks, Coach."

Others just looked at me. It was almost as if they didn't know what to say. I could sense that no man had spoken those words to some of these boys in a long time, and they did not know how to respond. I wish I could properly express the feeling that was among that group that night.

I don't know why, in our society, it is so taboo for boys to express their true emotions. There comes an age when our sons no longer are greeted by their fathers with a hug, but rather with a handshake. I think many fathers would have a hard time remembering when the last time was that he had verbally expressed the love that he felt for his teenage son. We all need to hear that. Love is ageless and timeless. I hope I never reach the point where I quit expressing that to my son. The natural response of most fathers is "He knows how I feel." I wonder if he does. Why don't you tell him?

That is why football is so great. It is okay for us to be emotional.

In fact, it is required. I only wish that all of our parents could be in the locker room with us before a big game so that they could see the emotion that their sons are able to express. They bare their hearts to their teammates and are unashamed about what others may think. Couldn't we train our sons to be better fathers and husbands by teaching them to be more expressive toward the ones they love? Our football team was based on love and respect for each other. That is what had brought us to that point.

Our pre-game talk to the players was short. What had started out as a selfish group of boys had developed into a family of mature young men. They knew what was expected of them and what had to be done. We had developed a custom of having the starting offensive and defensive teams form a circle in the locker room. The coaches would charge the players with their responsibilities of that night, and then the players, one by one, would have to look their neighbor in the eye and tell him what he could be counted on to do. There was something about saying it to each other that made them more committed to following through on their pledge. We reminded them that we were proud of them no matter what happened on the field. We asked them to leave their rocks in the locker room and to hang together during tough times. Nothing more needed to be said.

It was obvious from the opening kickoff that we were ready to play ball. We had possession of the ball first and began to pound away at the Green and White Rocks' defense. We were able to move the ball quickly down the field and were threatening to score when we were stopped by a holding penalty. More games are usually lost by your own mistakes than are ever won by your great plays. If you can control your mistakes, you greatly increase your chances of winning. We had blown a great opportunity to jump on top.

Our defense was just as fired up. Dublin was forced to punt on their first possession, and we were quickly back in control of the ball. On fourth and eight from our own twenty-five yard line, we were forced to punt. We had noticed from film studies of Dublin that when they went for an all out punt rush, they did not leave anyone to cover the pass. We had put in a call that our punter was to make at the line of scrimmage. If we saw Dublin line up in an all out rush, we would call out "Rock it." That meant that our two ends were to go out for a pass, and our punter was to throw the ball. We were sure that it would work, but it would be risky to do it from this deep in our own territory.

As we lined up, Dublin walked nine men up to the line of scrimmage. They were going for the block.

"Rock it," I screamed, from the sideline. "Rock it."

Our punter, Fishman, looked at me like I was nuts, so did Zach Korns, the receiver. "Fake a punt? This deep in our own territory?" they must have thought.

"Rock it." I called a third time.

When the ball was snapped, Dublin stormed through to block it. It was amazing to watch Mike softly toss the ball to Zach as nine green Dublin defenders charged the other way. Korns caught the ball and ran for a thirty yard gain. Their punt-return man was able to angle him toward the sideline and run him out of bounds. Zach came within six inches of a seventy-five yard touchdown off a fake punt. We had just sent Dublin a huge message that we had come to play!

Our team was fired up and in complete control of the game. We continued to move the ball down the field only to fumble it away to Dublin at the twenty yard line. We had made our second big mistake. Even though we had dominated the game early and should have been up 14-0, we had squandered two great opportunities and had nothing to show for our early game dominance. I was leery because I could not see Dublin allowing us to continue moving the ball the way we had. We had not made the most of our opportunities.

We stressed to our football team the importance of handling the sudden change. That is a situation where everything is going our way and then something happens to change the momentum. That fumble was a sudden change. We had to keep them from using this break as a stepping stone to an emotional swing. We had them back on their heels, and now we let them off the mat. Our defense did a great job and forced them to punt the football back to us. We took over on our own twenty and were determined not to be stopped this time.

On our first play, we tried to throw a quick pass, but we had a blocking mistake. One of their linemen burst through and hit our quarterback from behind just before he could throw the ball. The hit caused him to fumble, and Dublin pounced on the ball at our eighteen yard line.

It was as if we were snake-bitten. I saw a noticeable sag in the posture of our players. They knew that we could not make this many mistakes and expect to win. We were not able to handle the sudden change again, and two plays later, Dublin scored. We had played hard, yet we found ourselves on the short end of a 7-0 score.

For the rest of the half, we were a team without confidence. Our offense went into low gear as all of the emotion had disappeared from our team. Dublin's confidence had risen, and they smelled blood. We did not gain a first down on either of our next two possessions of the half. In between those possessions, Dublin had put together a well executed 75 yard march for a score. Their two point conversion made it 15-0. We weren't dead, but we were gasping for air.

I just hoped that we could make it to half-time without the roof falling in. With less than a minute to go, we got the ball back on our own thirty. I wasn't about to do anything foolish, so I called a running play just to run out the clock. There was a mix up on the hand-off, and Dublin fell on our third fumble of the first half. We could not afford to give up another score. If we went to the locker room down 15-0, we could sell the kids on the fact that we only needed to score twice to win the game. Even a field goal would force us to score a third time.

Dublin ran two plays and then lined their all-conference kicker up for a forty yard field goal. We stood helplessly on the sideline as we watched his kick sail low and wide to the left. As I saw the kick drift into the dark night, I glanced at the big electronic score-board which flashed the score. Dublin 15. London 0. The patient was sick, but still had a pulse. I was never so glad to see a halftime come in my life.

The players always made it into the locker room before the coaches did. I usually walked in slowly so that I was able to gather my thoughts and think about what I was going to say about the first half. This time I ran. I knew that I needed to get to the locker room before the rocks started to fly. We could not let something happen in the locker room that would destroy our unity for the rest of the game. I burst in, not knowing what to expect.

"Don't you start throwing those stones," I screamed. "We couldn't play any worse than we did in that first half. Keep your mouths shut and think about what you can do better in the second half. This game is not over. Get a drink and go to the bathroom. Give the coaches a chance to get together."

We stepped outside into the tunnel that runs under the stands. All year long, I felt that our coaches had done a tremendous job of adjusting at halftime. We were always able to make some change that would make a difference in the game. I turned to Coach Collier and Coach Shirley who were up in the press box during the game.

"What adjustments do we need to make? Why aren't we moving the ball"? I asked.

"Coach, we have moved the ball," Mark said as he took off his red hat and ran his hand through his thinning hair. "We've just got to stop making so many mistakes. We're beating ourselves."

I knew that, but it was great to hear someone else say the same thing. These were not "Yes" men I had surrounded myself with. They spoke what was on their minds. I turned to Coach Emmets.

"What about defense, Norm. What do we need to do?"

"I think we're playing well," he replied. "Except for that one drive, they haven't moved the ball at all. We've turned the ball over to them three different times. Let's just get them together and get them to do what they are supposed to do."

I really trusted this big man and his years of experience. Our game plan was sound. The worst thing we could do would be to abandon it and do something drastic.

"You guys may think I'm nuts," I said, "but we're going to win this game. We're better than they are. Let's go convince the kids of that."

We returned confidently and enthusiastically to the players. Our locker room was different from any one that I had ever been in. The players were sitting around in groups quietly talking among themselves. I didn't know if they believed that we could come back and win, but we had 24 minutes to reach our dreams. We gathered them together, made a few minor offensive and defensive adjustments and got ready to go on the field.

"Do you think that twenty-one points is too much for us to score in a half?" I asked without giving them time to answer. "All we have to do is stay together. There are no adjustments to make. Let's just play ball."

A final thought hit me before I let them go.

"We have got to stop them on their first drive this half. Let's grab the momentum back. We've come too far to give up now."

On the way out to the field, I reminded God of the promise He had made to me that night in church, the promise that we would win our last three games. I knew that His Word was true, and that He had not changed His mind.

The second half of that football game we were a different team. On Dublin's third play of the half, Zach Korns intercepted a pass that was thrown out near the Dublin sidelines, and that put us in business at mid-field. Our offense took the field, and, for the next sixteen minutes, put on the most incredible offensive display that I have ever been associated with.

It took us six plays to travel the fifty yards for our first score. Our attempt for two points missed and we trailed 15-6. That meant we still needed to score two more times to win the game.

That touchdown did wonders for us. It restored our confidence and an inspired defense took the field to get the ball back for us.

The emotion had returned to our sidelines as guys were patting each other on the back and yelling out words of encouragement.

With a renewed bounce in our step, we went to work. Our defense became a swarm of red helmets and white jerseys. It was three downs and punt, and our offense was back on the field.

On the previous drive we had discovered a chink in Dublin's armor, and we now went at them full bore. Because of his size, they had no one who could cover Curtis. Several times we threw the ball over the middle of the defense to see it somehow end up cradled in the safety of his large black hands. We strategically passed the ball to him, mixed in the run and easily drove seventy yards for a touchdown. When the kick sailed through the uprights, we were only a field goal away from the lead. There was pandemonium on our sideline.

When you spot someone fifteen points, you cannot afford to make any mistakes if you plan to get back into the game. We were in high gear now, and we knew that there was no way that Dublin could stop us. Unfortunately, we were celebrating too much.

On the ensuing kickoff, which was the last play of the third quarter, we allowed Dublin to return the ball 75 yards for a score. They kicked the point-after and suddenly we trailed 22-13. Just that quickly, we had allowed Dublin to get all of the momentum back. It was a stunned group of players that gathered around me after that score.

"Get your heads up," I yelled over the sound of our loudly-playing band. "They can't stop us. That touchdown only means we are going to have to score two more times. Quit feeling sorry for yourself. We scored twice last quarter, let's just do it again."

We started the fourth quarter on our own thirty-three yard line, and I knew we needed to score quickly to get the momentum back. After two running plays got us a first down, I decided to go for broke.

"Pro Right 750 Z flag," I said to the player carrying the play in. It was a play action pass, fake run to the left with a pass coming back to the right toward our sideline. I knew that they would be looking for the ball to go to Curtis, but this pass was to John Raffmeyer, the other receiver.

Moving John to this position was one of the more controversial moves we had made all year. At 6', 190 pounds, he was one of the strongest and fastest kids that we had. He had always been a running back, but after our first scrimmage, I had asked him to move to wide receiver so that we could develop a more balanced outside threat. Although I know he wanted to be the tailback, he agreed to make the move. During the first half of the season, we did very little passing and I know he felt that the move was not important. Since the Big Walnut game, he had begun to get better and so had our offense. He jogged in front of me as he returned to the huddle.

"Raff," I yelled as I gave him the thumbs up sign. "Beat him deep."

He looked at me and nodded. Our eyes met though the bars on his face-mask, and I saw a look of confidence.

The play worked to perfection. Our quarterback lofted a perfect strike as John shielded off the defender with his body. He extended his hands, brought the pass in, and scurried down the sidelines for a 46-yard touchdown pass. The extra-point kick was missed, but we had cut the score to 22-19. It had taken us one minute and thirty-six seconds to score.

I grabbed Coach Emmets by the shirt. There was bedlam all around us.

"Get us the daggone ball back. They can't stop us," I pleaded.

"I know that," he said excitedly. "We'll get it for you," he yelled as he ran down the sidelines with his arms flailing in exhortation.

Our defense was wild. We had bodies flying all over the place. Our kids were playing like wild men, and there was nothing that Dublin could do about it. After three downs, Dublin had to punt the ball back to us, and we took over eighty yards away from pay dirt.

We ran the ball on our first two plays, and Dublin held us to one yard. It was the first time all half that they had even come close to shutting us down. It was third and nine from our own twenty-one with seven minutes to go in the game. We could not afford to give them the ball back.

"634 and up," Coach Collier said over the headphones. "They are jumping all over Curtis, and no one is picking up Raff."

I sent in the play and watched as the safety stepped up to cover Curtis over the middle. Joe gave a fake as if to throw it to him, and then hit John streaking down the sidelines. Right in front of our bench he hauled the pass in, and tip-toed gingerly out of bounds. It was first and ten at our own forty-six yard line.

It was as if God was calling our plays. Whatever play we called seemed to work. When Dublin was looking for the run, we passed, and when they were expecting the pass, we ran. It took us six plays to be first and goal on their eight yard line. On first down, I called a pass.

"Pro right, quick right, X slant." I held my breath. It was the exact same pass play that had caused the argument between Curtis and I in practice earlier that week. I prayed to myself.

"Thank you, Jesus, for clear thinking."

The defense lined up exactly like they had in practice that day. I hoped that Curtis had listened. I focused on Curtis and saw him fake to the outside, cut hard to the inside, and reach up and pull in the pass for the go-ahead touchdown. Then I spotted the yellow flag. Our quarterback's mouthpiece had popped out of his mouth as he barked the signals. The referee threw a flag for improper equipment, and the score was nullified.

We could have buckled under, but we were not to be denied. We came back with the same play two plays later, and Dublin's defensive back interfered trying to get through Curtis' big frame to knock the pass down. That made it first and goal from the seven. Three plays later Joe sneaked the ball in from the one for the go-ahead score. The electronic scoreboard flashed 4:34 left in the game.

We lined up for the all important extra point. If we made it, it would require them to score a touchdown to win. Without it, a field goal would tie. The snap was accurate, the hold was good, and the kick split the uprights as the scoreboard danced in the background, "London 26 - Dublin 22."

The sideline was unbelievable. Guys were running around, jumping up and down, screaming at the tops of their lungs. Our stands had begun to empty as fans waited to charge onto the field, being held back by a chain-link fence that encircled the track. Out of the corner of my eye, I saw Coach Byard lying on the ground, kicking in excitement.

My insides were bursting. I wanted to scream and rejoice over where God had taken us, but I knew that there was plenty of football left to be played. Coach Emmets tried to settle the defense down and get their heads back into the game. It would be devastating to let this game slip away.

When Dublin got the ball, they were seventy yards from a score. Our defense had been overpowering the second half, but now they were too busy celebrating to get lined up properly. The noise from our crowd and from our sidelines was so loud that the players could not hear what we were yelling to them from the sideline.

The Rocks' offense began to pick us apart as they quickly moved the ball down the field. Our defense stiffened and they were faced with fourth and thirteen at the thirty.

"Watch the screen," Coach Emmets yelled above the din of the crowd.

The Dublin quarterback dropped back and threw the ball over the middle. It was hard to believe that the ball squeezed between our two linebackers, but the receiver caught it and fell to the ground at the fourteen yard line. First and ten, Dublin. One minute, fifteen seconds of agony left.

Dublin completed a short pass for no gain and then ran a draw which Ben Stronger smothered at the eleven yard line. They were forced to call their last timeout with twelve seconds left.

Before Coach Emmets ran onto the field he came over to me. "Anything special you want me to do?" he asked as he wrapped his big arm around me. I looked up into his round, expressive face. I thought of all we had been through together and the sacrifices he had made.

"Yeah," I grinned. "Stop them."

He smiled, slapped me on the back and charged onto the field, hitching-up his sagging pants, to call the biggest play of the season.

"Get the outside-linebackers wider," Mark Collier screamed into my headset. "They are just going to throw it out in the flat to one of the backs and we don't have anyone out there."

The thoughts were bouncing around in my head, and I was doing my best to gain control of the situation. Our sideline was frantic, and Coach Collier was screaming in my ear as we tried to come up with a defensive scheme that would halt this last minute drive.

"Korns needs to be wider, and so does Curtis," Mark screamed over the phones.

I was praying, as I always do through the game, and the commotion only seemed to be breaking the flow of my spirit.

"Tighten Carl up. He's giving up too much ground," Mark yelled.

I knew that the play on the field was out of our hands. We had prepared the team, and it was too late for adjustments to be made. Coach Collier's exhortations were distracting, and they were irritating my spirit.

"Mark, just shut up and pray," I blurted out to him.

His reply still echoes in my head.

"I already am."

I dropped to one knee to watch this final play unfold. The Dublin quarterback took the snap, rolled to his right, stopped, and threw the ball over the middle to a receiver breaking toward the goal line. My heart leapt.

Our safety, Doug Browning, was hanging in the middle, with his eyes focused on the quarterback. He moved forward, cut to his right, and stepped in front of the receiver as the ball settled into his arms for the game-winning interception.

The eastern half of the Dublin stadium erupted. Parents and students stormed onto the field in a sea of red and white. Our sidelines went berserk. Players were tackling teammates and rolling on the ground in joy. We had done the impossible.

London High School was the 1990 Central Buckeye League Champion!

OUTRIGHT

Ephesians 2:8-9 "For by grace are ye saved through faith; and that not of yourselves: it is the gift of God: Not of works, lest any man should boast."

The events immediately following the Dublin game are foggy. As time expired in that game, it seemed as if the whole town of London had descended upon the football field. It was the single most exhilarating moment that I had ever experienced in an athletic event. It was great to move among the crowd and receive hugs and congratulations from friends and strangers alike. Somewhere during the two months, we had truly become London's football team.

I cannot describe the satisfaction that I received from standing back and watching our football players bask in the glory of what they had accomplished. Their classmates were on the field slapping them on the back, and of course, they were receiving hugs from all of the pretty girls. All pre-season prognosticators had expected us to be no better than next to last in our division. Now we were on the top of the heap. For more than a year, I had preached to these young men that if they would be willing to sacrifice for the good of the team, great things would happen. As I stood on the field, I knew that what they had given up was nothing in comparison to what they had gained.

I don't know why we are so unwilling to put our trust in the Lord. Man, for some reason, seems to think that he has all of the answers. In Genesis, God said that man was made in His image. Somehow we have turned this whole thing around. We have put God into a little box and made Him conform to the image that we have of Him. If we would merely submit our lives and our will unto Him, we would be able to see Him as He really is. To know His true nature is to understand the good and perfect gifts that He has in store for us.

So many of us lead our lives on what we think God is. The Bible says in Malachi 3:6 "For I am the Lord, I change not;" What does change is our impression of Him. The Bible says that He is the same yesterday, today and forever. That is a great comfort to me. I understand that my situation may change, my circumstances may change, my attitude or health may change, but Jesus Christ will remain the same in the midst of the storm around me. More than anything, I have come to appreciate that football season for what it was: Proof positive in my life that all things are subject to change. 2 Corinthians 4:18 says "while we look not at the things which are seen, but at the things which are not seen, for the things which are seen are temporal, but the things which are not seen are eternal." By looking at things with our natural eye, focusing only on what we could see, there would have been no way that this season could have been predicted. A strong faith and belief in God and things which can't be seen had enabled this team to accomplish the impossible.

It would be so easy for me, our coaches, or our players to take the credit for what had happened. For fifteen years London High School had struggled to win a league championship and had done so in vain. To the natural eye, the circumstances had not changed. In fact, the climate for success may have gotten worse. Years and years of losing had convinced the players and the community that they were no good. Yet, here we were a year later, champions. What had happened? God had smiled upon us. He touched us with His never-changing presence, and in doing so, we were changed. Only by renewing our mind, something which you could not see, were we able to change the circumstances around us.

Always before, we had tried to do it the opposite way. We tried to change the circumstances so that the climate would be more likely to produce success. No matter what kind of soil you are planting in, if the seed is no good, you will not reap a harvest. We had taken hard, un-tillable soil and planted the perfect, never changing seed of the Word of God into it and now had reaped the greatest harvest in fifteen years. No man can take credit for that.

When we returned from Dublin that night, we were shocked to see hundreds of our fans waiting to greet us. The entire parking lot at the high school had been circled by parked cars. Each one of the cars had turned on their emergency flashers and as we turned the corner into the school, the flashing lights flickered in the dark night. It was almost as if our fans did not want this feeling to end.

We had made plans to build our mountain of rocks when we returned to the school. Because of the excitement and the chaos at the school, we were not able to formally do it. As I dismissed the players that night, I asked them to bring their rocks to school on Monday, and we would have a ceremony then. Many of the players objected. They felt that even though we had talked about the stone memorial, they would rather keep the rock as a reminder of this game. I agreed that they could keep them. I put my rock down in the soil outside the locker room and many of the athletes followed suit until we had created a pile of about twenty-five rocks.

I was more struck by those who chose to keep the rocks. 2 Corinthians 3:2-3, "Ye are our epistle written in our hearts, known and read of all men: Forasmuch as ye are manifestly declared to be the epistle of Christ ministered by us, written not with ink, but with the Spirit of the living God; not in tables of stone, but in fleshy tables of the heart.

The impact of the message had been inscribed into their hearts, and I knew that their lives were changed.

Our season was still was not over. We had won a share of the championship with our victory over Dublin, but we still had to beat Marysville in order to win the league title outright. Although the game was somewhat anti-climactic, it was still necessary for us to take care of business.

Marysville was a town that a few years ago had been very similar to London. It is the county seat of Union County and is twenty-five miles north of London. For years the financial base of Marysville had been farming and prisons. Marysville is the home to one of the major correctional facilities for women in the state of Ohio. In the late 70's Marysville received a real shot in the arm when Honda of America built their first American car plant just west of town. This brought in a major influx of people and changed the image of the town. Because of the growth, Marysville would be moving to a larger league next year. They have just moved into a large, new high school. Marysville's nickname is the Monarchs. A monarch is a type of lion, but our kids jokingly call Marysville the "Butterflies".

Marysville was only one game behind us. If they were to beat us, we would end up tied for the championship with them. As we viewed them on film, it became apparent to all of the coaches that we were the better team. Our concern, once again, was the mental condition of our football team. The emotional victory over Dublin and subsequent back-slapping by our fans made us very ripe for an upset. Add to that the fact that Marysville was very excited about the prospects of a championship, and all of the elements were present for a great championship football game.

The maturity of our football team was evident that week. The first thing I did at Monday's practice was show the players a large safety pin that I was wearing in my hat. The pin was exceptionally large and I stuck it through the front of my red hat. Periodically I would remove the pin and feign popping a balloon whenever an athlete gave some indication of self-satisfaction. I called it my "head poppin' pin" to be used to deflate anyone who we felt was bigheaded. The kids got the message and chuckled good naturedly about my pin.

It was the most relaxed group of football players that I had ever coached. They were relaxed, not in an overconfident sense, but in a confident, business-like sense. Whereas the previous week had been one of arguments and emotional outbursts, this week was subdued and focused. I couldn't help but think back to the third week of the season when we had been sky high and lost to West Jefferson because of the attitude that West Jefferson had shown against us. This week we had that air of confidence that West Jefferson had shown.

Something else had popped into the picture. For the first time in London history, we had a chance to make the State football playoffs. This was something that very few teams in Ohio get the opportunity to do. If we were to win our last game, and if the right teams around the state lost, we could receive that fourth and final playoff spot. That was some added incentive for our football team, something that we had never considered possible a few months before.

As we boarded the bus for Marysville that Friday evening, I was completely confident that we were going to win the game. After nine games, I had learned how to read our kids, and I had never seen their attitude more perfect for what they had to do. It was on the way to the game that I received the inspiration to write this book.

The night before, at our Thursday night meal, I had asked Coach Emmets to deliver our final message to the team. We gathered again in the same auditorium that had been so special to us all year. He spoke eloquently and from the heart as he took all of us back through the football season. He started with our two-a-day practices, and led us step by step through this remarkable season.

He brought to our remembrance so many things that we had all lost sight of. We talked of the obstacles that we had faced and described just how we had overcome them. Coach Emmets is a very energetic, enthusiastic man, but this night he spoke with solemnity. It was inspiring and really put things into perspective.

As I rode on the bus towards Marysville, I looked out the windows at the acres and acres of flat grain fields and reflected on just how God had blessed us. Many times over my life when something amazing or hard to believe would happen I would say, "I could write a book." On this crisp, cool October evening, that very thought popped into my head again.

"I should write a book," went my thoughts as I stared out the window at an old wooden covered bridge sagging against the autumn horizon.

"Go ahead," came another thought that I know was not mine.

"Yeah! I'll write a book," my mind said again. "But what will I call it?"

"Ordered by the Lord," came the matter-of-fact thought.

"Okay, I'll do it," I said to myself.

That was it. The book was born in my mind. Someone once told me that you would never forget where you were when God spoke to you. It is a moment of time stamped in my brain. I could take you on the highway and show you the exact corn field we were passing when the inspiration came.

How do I know it was God? What did His voice sound like? Do I hear from Him often? Those are all questions that you may want to ask. I can't answer any of them, but I know it was Him. I guess I shouldn't be so surprised. After all, God is not out in the great beyond somewhere. He is alive within my heart. Come to think of it, He wouldn't have to speak very loudly for me to hear Him, would He?

When we arrived at Marysville I shared with a couple of the coaches outside the locker room that I was going to write a book and what the name of it was going to be. I didn't tell them to be bragging, but rather to confirm to God that I was not ashamed to confess my vision before men. Once I said it, I was committed to doing it.

All during our pre-game warm-up, I moved about our team praying in the spirit. I had never done that before, but I felt a strong leading from the Holy Spirit that this was what I should do. I didn't know why, but I could sense a need to intercede.

As we were leaving the field for our last minute preparations, one of our freshmen coaches, Scott McKinney, came up to me. He was a young man who was very spiritually attuned, and we had counseled together several different times during the season. Scott and I were on the same wavelength spiritually.

Scott is not a teacher. He is a mechanic. As he likes to say, he fixes things. He is always willing to do anything that he can to help and this includes telling me what he senses in his spirit. Scott played football at London during the glory years of the late 60's. At 5'10", 185 pounds, he had stayed youthful and physically fit and is very knowledgeable in weight lifting.

"Coach," he said, "I sense the presence of that same spirit that was on our freshmen last night." Our freshmen had played their worst football game of the year the night before and the coaches had explained after the game that the kids had played in a state of confusion.

"What do you mean, Scott?" I asked as I looked into his concerned face.

"That spirit of confusion," he continued. "It was all over our team and we could not get them straightened out."

"We're okay, Scott," I said confidently. "I've been praying out on the field all through warm-ups."

"Well, all right, but I really feel its presence," he said uneasily.

As we continued to walk toward the locker room, I heard that soft still voice again.

"Pray." I concentrated on the thought a second.

"Pray the prayer of agreement," the thought returned. The prayer of agreement is found in Matthew 18:19. "Again I say to you, that if two of you agree on earth about anything that they may ask, it shall be done for them by My Father who is in heaven."

"Let's pray about it, Scott," I said. "Take my hand." I took Scott's weathered hand, and as we continued to walk toward the locker room, we offered the prayer of agreement. We prayed boldly and openly as we made our way off of the field. We were oblivious to those around us. I can only wonder what they must have thought. We completed the prayer just before we joined the team and we looked at each other knowing that we had headed off the enemy. All during the warm-up, my spirit had been alerted to the danger as I prayed in the midst of our team, but Scott's spirit had given witness to me that we had not done enough. The prayer of agreement was all that was needed to break the back of the enemy.

Things seem to be going well in the locker room, but as we gathered the team together for our pre-game prayer, I was distracted by a commotion in the back of the locker room.

"Put someone in for me, Coach. I can't catch the ball." It was Curtis.

"What are you talking about, Curtis?" I said. "You're all right."

"I'm telling you, you better start Doug. I can't play tonight." he said as fear choked off his voice.

"What's wrong with you, man?" said a teammate.

"Shut up and get out there," said another. "Leave me alone, Man." he screamed. "I'm telling you, Coach. Get someone else in there. I can't catch tonight. I dropped everything during warm-ups."

"Relax, Curtis. We'll talk about it in a minute." I answered.

I could not let this affect the rest of the team. I knew what needed to be done, but could I do it now? I circled up the team for our pre-game prayer. I charged them with what they needed to do and what waited for us at the end of the game. They burst from the locker room ready to bring home the outright championship.

All, that is, except for Curtis.

I moved toward the corner where he was slumped over in the dimly lit hallway, surrounded by lockers.

"Are you all right, big fella?" I asked.

"I don't know what is wrong," he said desperately. I looked at this little boy in this man's body, and I was filled with compassion.

"Curtis," I paused. "Can I pray for you?"

Tears filled his eyes as he looked at me. He nodded yes, and remained kneeling.

I reached out my hand and laid it upon his head.

"Oh, Jesus, we praise you for the many talents and abilities that you have brought to this young man. We thank you for his health and for having brought all of us together for this great season. I ask you now, Father, that you send your Holy Spirit upon this young man, that you will fill him with power and confidence to do the job that you have appointed him to do. I take authority over any spirits that may try to keep him from what rightly belongs to him, and in the name of Jesus Christ, I command them to be gone. Father, we thank you and praise you for what you have done and we send this young man forth to perform as you would want him to. In Jesus' name, Amen."

Tears rolled down his cheeks as he stood up and fastened his chin strap. I could sense that he had been delivered from that oppression, and we hurried out together to join his teammates who were milling around wondering what had become of their coach. We huddled up one last time before the kickoff team charged onto the field.

The first half resembled a fast-break basketball game. It had to be fun to watch. It did not take long for us to establish the fact that we had come to play ball. On our second play from scrimmage, our Joey Bronson broke loose on a sixty-five yard run. He was angled out of bounds at the ten yard line, but we scored on the very next play. Any concern about our not being ready to play went out the window right there.

After we fumbled on our next possession, Marysville drove the ball thirty-five yards for the tying score. We knew that we needed to answer in a hurry.

The Red Raiders put together a nice scoring drive to again take the lead. The drive was aided by two receptions by Curtis, who only minutes before was convinced he couldn't play. On the ensuing kick-off, we were able to recover the short, squib kick. One play later, Joe lofted a perfect strike down the middle to Curtis for a 38-yard touchdown pass. I felt a great deal of joy as Curtis reached up with his large hands and hauled the pass in. With eight minutes to go in the half, we were on top 21-7. It looked like a rout was on. Unfortunately, I guess our players thought that a rout was on as well. Marysville was able to score twice in the last few minutes of the half.

The first score was set up by a seventy yard run by Marysville's quarterback. We missed a couple of tackles and watched him zigzag down the field. He cut in and out from behind his blue clad teammates, and we finally knocked him out at the five yard line. Three plays later, the Monarchs scored.

In the final minute of the first half, they were able to score again. The final blow was a twenty-eight yard touchdown pass that deserved to be on any football highlight show. On fourth down and eighteen and ten seconds left in the half, the Marysville quarterback dropped back to pass. We put on a tremendous rush and forced him to retreat about fifteen yards. As three of our defenders swarmed on top of him, he somehow stepped out of one tackle, ducked out from under another, and squirted out from the middle of them. He scrambled to his left, and as he was being tackled, threw the ball to his fullback who was all alone in the right flat. He caught the ball and raced down the far sidelines. Our safety finally angled him off at the goal line and knocked him out of bounds. The striped-shirted referee ruled that he had crossed the goal line before being driven out and raised his arms skyward. With no time left on the clock, we blocked the extra point for a 21-20 halftime lead. So much for a rout.

Things were calm at halftime as we gathered in the cramped, overheated locker room. Our kids knew that we were the better team and that we had allowed them to get back into the game. We had the ball first to start the second half, and we emphasized the importance of scoring and taking them out of the game. To do this, I had decided to use a trick play.

Our first play would be a double pass. That was a play where the quarterback threw the ball sideways to one of our receivers, Raffmeyer, who then threw it down the field to our tight end. To work the play better, we inserted Carl Kingsley into the game, the fastest sophomore on our team. He went in at tight end, and the pass would be thrown to him. I informed Carl of what we were going to do before we left the locker room. That was a mistake.

We ran the play to perfection. Marysville took the fake, and Carl found himself twenty-five yards behind their nearest defender. Raffmeyer saw how open Carl was and threw the ball very high so that Carl would have the chance to settle under it. The ball seemed to take an eternity to come down as it drifted slowly, silhouetted against the dark, night sky. When it did, it bounced in and out, in and out, and in and out of Carl's hands as he fell to the turf trying to juggle the ball into his control. He could not hang on.

I felt badly for him because I knew that he was embarrassed, and he felt that he had let the team down. I knew that it was my fault. By telling him about the play so early, I had given him too much time to think about it. He became nervous as he waited for the second half to begin. When he found himself as wide open as he was, he became anxious. It is the toughest pass to catch. If you are covered closely, you don't have time to think. You merely react. Carl knew that all he had to do was catch the football, and he would have a touchdown. As the pass dropped out of the sky, it must have looked as big as a hot-air balloon, and he tried to run before he caught it. He was a fine player, a starter on defense as a sophomore, and he would make many great plays for us in the future.

This could have been a big let-down. An obvious touchdown had literally slipped through our fingers. Instead, we buckled up our chin straps and put together a backbreaking seventy yard drive for a score. The drive consumed almost eight minutes of the third quarter as we pounded away at them up the middle and then sneaked Joey around the end. The touchdown was scored when

Joey threw a perfect eight yard pass to John Raffmeyer in the far corner of the end zone. It took away any momentum that Marysville might have gained in the first half.

Our defense stiffened and shut them out during the second half. When Joe completed a forty-three yard touchdown pass to Raffmeyer midway through the fourth quarter, we put the wraps on our miracle championship season. As the clock wound down, we stormed onto the field to celebrate our 35-20 victory.

Just as they had done the previous week at Dublin, our fans joined us for the on- field celebration. Although the victory had not been as dramatic, it was very fulfilling to realize that no one would be able to take it from us now. After previous games, we had to worry about next week's game. That night, joy and relief poured out of our kids. It truly had been a Cinderella story. Winning our last six games was incredible, but what made it more amazing was that we had played four of our last five games on the road. Nothing about it had been easy.

Of all the memories of that season, nothing was more poignant than what occurred on that field after the game. As was our custom, I tried to get the players to circle up for our post-game prayer. There was so much bedlam on the field that this was nearly impossible. It was a replay from the week before with seemingly the entire town of London on the field. After several minutes, I was able to get the attention of enough of the players to get them to form a circle. However, in the midst of our group were parents, brothers and sisters, aunts, uncles, grandparents, friends, and just plain old fans. I was not leaving the field until we did what we had done after every game, give thanks to our Creator, but how could we do it with all of these people in the midst of us.

"Listen up," I yelled. The crowd grew silent and closed in around me.

"We never leave the field without taking time to thank God for what He has given us. Our football team would be honored if you would care to join us for the Lord's Prayer."

As I waited for everyone to prepare themselves, I was given a short vision of what God must have been thinking. In my mind's eye, I was hovering above the field looking down at literally hundreds of people joining together for a moment of thanks. Players and fans joined hands and wrapped arms around each other's shoulders in one accord. It was an inspiring moment.

Was this the purpose for God sending this great season? When was the last time London had seen people of all ages, colors, economic backgrounds, and walks of life join together in a public place in prayer? Was God sending us a message? I believe that He was. He wants to change us. He can help us if we will just turn to Him. That season was about more than a football game. It involved destiny and eternity. It was for every citizen in London. 2 Chronicles 7:14 states "If my people, which are called by my name, shall humble themselves, and pray, and seek my face, and turn from their wicked ways; then will I hear from heaven, and will forgive their sin, and will heal their land."

Thank you, Jesus. Help us to see.

HUMPTY DUMPTY

Isaiah 3:10 Say ye to the righteous, that it shall be well with him: for they shall eat the fruit of their doings."

It had been an unbelievable year. No one could have imagined how far we would go. Our football team had been restored from out of the ashes, and, for the first time in fifteen years, we were sitting on top of the heap. Our team had become the talk of the town and everyone had an explanation about who was responsible for our resurgence. I knew that our season had been the work of God. All God had done was to use the things that were available to Him to work a miracle.

With the victory over Marysville our team was 8-2. We had won our last six football games, just as Zach Korns had spoken 6 weeks earlier, and we now stood on the threshold of our first-ever state football playoff appearance. Although it would take the right combination of wins and losses from some other teams, it seemed like that would be the crowning achievement to this miracle season.

As we began to check scores on Saturday morning, it was astounding to see that everything was falling our way. Teams ahead of us in the ratings were being upset, and it appeared to be coming down to one final game on Saturday night. If the right team won, we would make the playoffs. We were all excited and made plans to go to Dayton to watch the game that evening.

As I was sitting at home preparing to go to the game, God let me know that we would not be going to the playoffs. The thought came out of nowhere as I was sitting on the edge of my bed putting on my shoes.

"Your season is over," came the thought.

I stopped and focused in on our oak-paneled bedroom wall, as I knew the thought was not from me.

"What do you mean?" I asked in my head.

"You are not going to the playoffs. Don't get your hopes up," came the response.

"Why not, God?" I half pleaded. "You have brought us this far, why not glorify Yourself by giving our team another first?"

"Because you didn't believe for it," He said. "It could have been yours but you didn't ask for it."

I knew exactly what He meant. A month before I had asked God to grant us victories in our last three games. He had granted that petition, but I now realized that I had not asked for enough.

When I had asked for those three victories, it seemed like an almost impossible thing to ask God to do. If I had more faith, I would have asked for us to make the playoffs or maybe to even win the state. However, my faith was only sufficient to ask for three more victories and the league championship. I didn't believe for any more than that.

God never changes. He is the great "I Am," the God of the present tense. He is constantly with us, and it is impossible for us to be someplace where He is not. He is the creator of the universe. He owns the cattle on a thousand hillsides. Nothing was made that He did not make.

I have come to understand that God can do anything. It doesn't matter what our opinion of God is; that doesn't change Him. He remains the same no matter what we think. Just because I don't think He can heal my body does not change the fact that He can. It only means I can't receive it. God is not limited by what He can do, but rather, by what we believe He can do. That is faith, believing something even though you can't prove it. Let me give this example.

I have been married to my beautiful wife for eleven years. There is nothing that we would not do for each other. I know that if I needed her to run to Columbus and pick something up for me that she would do it. I have faith in her. Even though she hasn't run the errand yet, I know that she will do it. All I have to do is ask. I know her. I know her nature. I know her love for me. If there was any way that she could do it, she would.

God is the same way. He loves me more than my wife does, and there is nothing that He would not do for me. Just like my wife, God can only do what I ask Him to do. Since God can do all things, and there is nothing that is impossible to Him, if I do not have enough faith in Him to ask for something, then there is no way that he can reward me. Mark 9:23 says "All things are possible to him that believeth." Believing is faith, knowing that it will happen even though it appears impossible.

Why don't we believe God more? Why do we have so little faith in Him? I think it is because we do not really know who He is. We do not understand His true nature. If we could see Him for who He really is, then we would understand what His power is. Do you really think that my wife is nicer than God? If she is willing to do things for me, then how much more willing must God be? I don't doubt my wife because I know her so well. Isn't it sad to think that I know my wife better than I know my Creator? He is waiting to do whatever I ask of Him. If I could only believe, then all things would be possible to me. Why? Because God makes all things happen, and there is nothing that He cannot do.

Why then, if God can do all things, does He not let me win the lottery? I believe it is because He is the God of the present tense. He knows the future as well as the past. He knows my heart, and

He knows my motives, and He will not grant me a prayer that will cause me harm or is out of His will. Simple, huh? Just how do you learn the will of God?

It all comes back to knowing Him. I would not ask my wife to drive to Columbus and buy some drugs for me. She would not do it. She knows what could happen to me if I were to get involved in drugs, and she would not play a part in my destruction. She loves me too much. God is the same way. He knows me and loves me, and He will not help me to destroy myself.

Our problem is not with God; it is with us. To truly know Him is to know His will for our lives. Without knowing Him, we cannot know His will. III John 2 says "Beloved, I wish above all things that thou mayest prosper and be in health, even as thy soul prospereth." Prospering is God's will for you. He wants you to prosper and be healthy, but only to the degree that you are prospering spiritually. Take care of your soul, and God will take care of the rest.

Whether or not you realize it, we all have faith. Some of us just use it differently. Does it take any more faith to believe that something good is going to happen, rather than something bad? Both are faith in something that hasn't happened yet. For many of us, it is easier to believe something negative than it is to believe something positive. It doesn't take any more faith to believe negatively, it is just faith that things won't turn out the way that we want them to. That is what Romans 12 means when it talks about renewing your mind. Stop having faith that bad things will happen. Believe for the best, and then stand firm.

We loaded up a van full of coaches and players and headed that evening to watch the game. Everyone was excited about the prospects of making the playoffs. I did not share with them my revelation, but I know that they could sense my apprehension.

It was a fun evening. For us to have any chance of making the playoffs, the underdog in that game needed to win. We sat on their side of the field and quickly learned that their fans were not very enthusiastic. To liven things up, some of our players began to lead cheers from the stands. Soon they were down in front with the cheerleaders rooting that team on to victory. The enthusiasm of the crowd began to pick up, and the team was spurred on to a come-from-behind, upset victory. It looked as though all of the things that we needed to make the playoffs had occurred.

Everyone was excited on the way back talking about who we would play and how much fun that would be. I could not share in the excitement because I knew that our season was over. I already knew God's answer.

The next evening the final answer was confirmed. We had missed the playoffs by two computer points. A team that we had not expected to win had pulled an upset that allowed another team to climb those two points above us. We had been close, but now the reality had set in. If one team that we had beaten during the course of the year would have won one more game during the season, we would have made the playoffs. It was that close. If only I had enough faith a month earlier, I am convinced that God would have caused that to happen. I learned to never sell the power of God short. From now on I will ask for the best, and I know that God will deliver.

It was very difficult to inform the team that our season was over. Over the course of the year, they had developed a trust in me. They knew that if I told them something, it must be true. They had seen God's miracle hand pull surprise after surprise. I had told them that we were going to make the playoffs, and I know that they believed me. Now I had to break the bad news to them.

We gathered in the gym where we had held so many of our meetings throughout the year. We discussed the season and all that we had accomplished. It was a proud group of young men in that room.

I thought back to the summer. I thought of the camping trip and the emotional meeting that took place in this same gym that we were now gathered in. It was as if this was a different group of boys. As I looked around the room at them, as they shot basketballs and joked with each other, I once again realized what a family we had become. Everyone milled around. It was as if we believed that if we hung around long enough, the state would change their minds and invite us to the playoffs. No one wanted this season to be over. It was a real lesson in life that all things must pass. Our season was over, but the memory of what we had done, what we had accomplished, and what we had become would live forever within each one of us.

Still, there will always be some question in my mind as to whether or not I have done enough. We only have the advantage of seeing things from our own perspective, and sometimes we do not give things a fair appraisal. If things are good for us, then we assume that everyone else feels the same way, too. That is not always the case. I know that not every player was happy with the season, but it is not my job to try and please everyone.

I had known all year long that I was walking a fine line with my Christian beliefs and just what I could share with the players. I did not want to force my beliefs on them, but at the same time, I wanted to share with them what I knew worked.

Just what is it about religion that scares people? I have fought battles within my own family over what God is doing in my life. I have heard people say "He got religion," as if it were some kind of disease. I honestly believe that some people would be less worried about me if I spent all of my time in a bar rather than in church. I do know this: even if there was no God and all of this Jesus stuff was a hoax, I would still choose to live my life by Christian values. Man has found no better way for people to live together than by the Golden Rule. That is just a paraphrasing of Matthew 22:37 "Jesus said unto him, Thou shalt love the Lord thy God with all thy heart, and with all thy soul, and with all thy mind. This is the first and great commandment. And the second is like unto it, Thou shalt love thy neighbour as thyself. On these two commandments hang all the law and the prophets."

Why would parents not want their children to be taught by these principles? I believe that most parents would. In our society the objection of one parent would be enough to force the administration to order me to stop sharing what I believe with the football team, regardless of how the other parents felt.

Whatever happened to freedom of speech? It is okay for kids to read pornography, for them to listen to the filth that disguises itself as rock music, or to spend hours sitting in front of the television because they are thinking human beings and are able to choose for themselves what they will believe. Why then is it not okay for a teacher to share his beliefs about God? Do these same bright children suddenly lose their ability to decide what they will or will not believe? That is the lie. Without the influence of teachers with strong moral character, our kids will be forced to accept as fact the information that they receive from those in whom they put their trust. Just who are those people? Madonna, AC/DC, 2-Live Crew? They may be sexy and play good music, but I doubt very much if most parents would want their kids to live their lives by the values that these rock stars espouse. Christians need to stand up and make their feelings known, or we will end up turning our kids over to the rock stars of the world. Has freedom of speech come to mean the right to talk about anything but God? Is it any wonder our schools are in such bad shape?

I was fully prepared for an attack against my right to teach what I believe. I was not forcing anyone to agree with me, I was just sharing what had worked in my own life. To not give them the information that I have would be to deprive them of an education. One of my science professors at Otterbein College believed in UFO's and enjoyed talking about them in class. That did not lead me to believe like him. He gave us the information and his opinion on it and then allowed us to make up our own minds. No matter how long he talked to me, he would not convince me.

Belief in God is the same way. No one should force someone to agree with them, but the information should be presented. I was prepared to sacrifice my job over this issue. The day that someone tries to tell me what I can talk about with the football team I coach, is the day that I am done coaching. It was God who put me in London, and He would let me know when the battle there was done.

At our end of the year football banquet, I received confirmation that I had touched the lives of our young men. It is customary for the football team to buy gifts for the coaches to be presented at the end of the season. Over the years I have received ties, shirts, sweaters, gift certificates and others. Nothing has ever touched me like the gift that I received from this team.

The banquet was held in the same auditorium where the players had met so many times before. This night they were joined by brothers and sisters, parents, girlfriends, and grandparents. The yellow theatre seats were nearly all taken. Our captains, Ben Stronger and Joe Bronson, called all of the coaches to the front of the room and presented each of us with a small box. In the box was a pocket knife with "1990 CBL Champs" engraved on the side. We were all touched and pleased by the memento that they had given us.

Ben then reached into the brown paper sack that he was carrying and lifted out a white box wrapped in red ribbon. He stepped to the podium and said, "Coach, on behalf of the team, I would like to present this to you for all that you have taught us this year."

I accepted the gift from Ben and then stepped to the podium to open it. With the same brown curtain as a background, I felt the eyes of everyone in that room upon me. I nervously opened the box. For a second, I froze. I was overwhelmed, and I felt a lump form in my throat. I pulled out the most precious gift that I had ever received. The gold letters jumped off of the black cover. THE RYRIE STUDY BIBLE.

I opened it up to find that it had been signed by the team. I was stunned. These young men were expressing, in the best way that they knew how, their thanks for all that had happened during the year. They were telling me that they had received the message that I was sending, and that they, too, knew that God had been at work in our lives. For the first time, I knew that they had accepted me for who I was, a coach who happened to be a Christian. But more than anything, they were telling me that they knew that I was not a phony.

I choked back the tears as I attempted to share my feelings. As I looked over this diverse crowd, I realized again that we are all God's people. The message that I was carrying was for everyone. The Holy Spirit did not leave me hanging, but rather brought to my memory a story that I had heard earlier.

"I have never received anything that means more to me than this." I felt a tear trickle down my cheek and took a deep breath to gather myself as the packed auditorium shuffled nervously.

"I know that you did not come here to hear me preach, but I want you to know that I have been aware of God's hand upon our team. I know that London has had a rough time in football the past few seasons, and everyone was grabbing at straws in an attempt to find the answer. It was nothing that I have done. It was a group effort. We became a team, a family, something that at times seemed impossible to do. I am reminded of the nursery rhyme, "Humpty-Dumpty," because I think it is fitting for our team.

"Humpty Dumpty sat on the wall, Humpty Dumpty had a great fall. All of the king's horses and all of the king's men, Couldn't put Humpty back together again."

I looked around the room at all the faces, young and old, that were looking back at me.

"The problem with Humpty was the same problem that we have had here at London. When things got bad, they called on all of the king's horses and all of the king's men, but there was nothing that the horses and men could do about it. They couldn't put things back together. Some things are out of our control. Here is the answer."

I picked up my shiny, new Bible and extended it towards the crowd.

"Here is the answer," I repeated, "Rather than calling the king's horses and the king's men, they should have called on the King."

WHAT'S NEXT?

Psalm 37:23 "The steps of a good man are ordered by the LORD: and he delighteth in his way."

It is not easy writing a book. In fact, the whole time that I have been writing, I have been fighting the feeling that I am not qualified to be doing this. I am not an expert in my field, nor have I done anything profound. What could I have to say that others might be interested in? I'm just a coach, an everyday guy. No different from hundreds of others that you know.

But that is just the point. I am no different than anyone else. What I have seen God do in my life can just as easily be done in yours. I speak humbly and honestly. I am an ordinary guy serving an extraordinary God.

My past is not squeaky clean. I have done more than my share of sinning. In fact, I am sure that many people may read this book and say, "Daubenmire, a Christian? Boy, I have heard it all. I remember when."

Our past is constantly there. We cannot escape it. Somebody

will always remember. I cannot control what others say or think.

That is the miracle of Jesus. The day that I accepted Him as my Lord and Savior is the day that I became a new person. 2 Corinthians 5:17 tells us "Therefore if any man be in Christ, he is a new creature: old things are passed away; behold, all things are become new." The old me is gone. The guy who did all of those foolish, sinful things, died the day that I asked Christ into my heart. I don't deny that I did them, but in the eyes of God, they are no longer visible. He sees only the sacrificial blood of His Son, Jesus Christ. That blood has cleansed me from my sins. I have been redeemed.

I have lived the life of sin, and I have lived as a Christian. I know both sides. The Christian life is harder, but it's much more fulfilling. My only regret is that I did not turn to Christ sooner.

My purpose in writing this book is not to brag about what a great coach I am, or to insinuate that I know God better than others. As I have already stated, I am no better than anyone else. I am a sinner who has found a savior. I want so much to be able to share the Good News of Jesus Christ with my fellow man.

Jesus Christ wants to enter your life as well. He wants to give you the power to overcome your problems. If you have never accepted Christ as your Lord and Savior, and you would like to know Him, simply repeat aloud the prayer below, and allow Him to become real in your life.

"Father, I come to you as a sinner in need of a Savior. I have committed sins, and I ask for your forgiveness. Enter into my heart, wash me clean of my sins, and give me a new start. I turn from my sinful ways, and reach out to you.

"Satan, I renounce you. You are not my God, and I will not serve you. Go from me now in the name of Jesus Christ.

"Heavenly Father, I will live my life for you as you show me how. In Jesus' name, Amen."

The whole issue of Jesus is about more than Heaven and Hell. We all possess a mortal soul, and when our physical body dies, that soul is going to live forever somewhere. Because of the sacrifice of

Jesus Christ, His paying our sin debt, we all have the opportunity to go to Heaven. It is not something that we earn, but rather it is a free gift for anyone who chooses to accept it.

However, Jesus can do more than give you eternal life. Our existence here on earth can be difficult. Everyday we face problems. Jesus came to earth and lived as a man so that He could experience first-hand what it was like to be a man. He suffered greater tribulation and persecution than any man who ever lived, so He understands what we have to go through. The purpose of His death was not only to win for us eternal life, but also to provide help for all of us while we are here on earth. His death and resurrection guarantees us power here and now, not just some reward in the great by and by.

My purpose is to share with everyone just what is available to them through the blood of Jesus Christ. No matter what the question, He is the answer. No matter the ailment, He is the cure. Man was not created to suffer. He was created to glorify and serve God. He is our Father. He loves us. He wants to do more for us than we could ever imagine. This book is a testimony to that fact. This football season was a miracle. It was a demonstration of what God wants to do in the lives of every one of us. If we could believe that, we would be free from all the weights of this world. John 8:32 says "And ye shall know the truth, and the truth shall make you free." Search God's Word, and you will find a loving, compassionate, ever-present God. He is reaching out to you.

So where does my life go from here? How do we top this story-book season? No matter how successful we are in the future, it will be difficult to outdo this season. There was a feeling and maturing among this group of young men that will be hard to duplicate. I take joy in knowing that God is not finished yet.

There are two powerful scriptures upon which I base my faith. They have altered the way that I see things and the way that I am able to handle disappointment.

The first one is Mark 9:23 "Jesus said unto him, If thou canst believe, all things are possible to him that believeth."

We need to lock in and get a revelation of who God is and what our relationship with Him is supposed to be. Once we can do that, once we can realize that He can and will do all things for us, then we will never again face a battle that we will not win. Believing is the key. We have to know Him to believe Him.

The second scripture that is important to me is Romans 8:28 "And we know that God causes all things to work together for good to those who love God, to those who are called according to His purpose." It does not matter what kind of trouble I encounter or what kind of mess I find myself in, God is able to take that situation and make good out of it. He doesn't promise everything will be good, only that He will make good out of it. All I have to do is believe that He is in control.

Sure, I may experience times when everything may seem to be going against me, but I am comforted by the fact that God is in control of my life. Whatever problem I face is just another chapter in the book that God is writing about my life. He knows the beginning and the end, and I have His promise that He will bring me out a winner.

There is a saying that I have heard.

"This day is God's gift to you. What you do with it is your gift to God."

I am excited about the future and the work that I can do for God. I have locked onto Psalm 37. "All setbacks are temporary. I was born to win. How can I fail? I have realized that my steps are ordered by the Lord."